GUNNERS AT THE BATTLEFRONT

GUNNERS AT THE BATTLEFRONT

Chhamb, Jelep La and Siachen

Lt Col Ashok Kumar Kher
with
Ravi Kher

PRABHAT
PRAKASHAN

Published by
PRABHAT PRAKASHAN PVT. LTD.
4/19 Asaf Ali Road,
New Delhi-110 002 (INDIA)
e-mail: prabhatbooks@gmail.com

ISBN 978-93-90923-26-7
GUNNERS AT THE BATTLEFRONT
by Lt Col Ashok Kumar Kher • Ravi Kher

Edition
2026

Price
₹ 600.00 (Rupees Six Hundred only)

Printed at
Shree Sai Printers, Sahibabad

Foreword

I feel honoured and privileged to write a foreword to the book titled, *Gunners at the Battlefront : Chhamb, Jelep La and Siachen*, which is a true narration and an honest account of the battles and operations with which Colonel AK Kher has been associated thoughout his journey in the 'Olive Green'.

My association with Col AK Kher goes back to the days when I was a young Captain with five years of service, performing the duties of an Adjutant of my battalion, 18 Kumaon while deployed in 'Op Meghdoot' during 1985-86 with then Major AK Kher as a Battery Commander of 39 Medium deployed at Post 9.

My unit held a vast area of sub-sector west from Turtuk to the southern glacier. Therefore, the unit always found itself grossly inadequate in resources, especially in terms of fire power. When it came to winning the race to occupy the dominating heights and saddles, we won hands down, but to make the enemy pay for any misadventure, we needed firepower with high trajectory weapons to strike deep into the enemy's side. Major AK Kher did just that.....

It was during June-July 1985 when I was on a course that 39 Medium Regiment was asked to deploy a troop of 130 mm guns in area Post 9, which was approximately 15 kms short of Turtuk. After our induction into the sub-sector in the west, covering the area from Turtuk to the southern glacier, in 1984, our Unit patrolled the glacier under the code name Rama. Post 9 was the place from where one had to climb up to the glacier. It had a sharp bend in the river, a Bailey bridge and a small, flat patch at the base of the hill, just above the Shyok river which may have been created by a landslide at some point in time. To deploy a Troop of 130 mm guns up the hill was seemingly an unachievable task but it was the only place which offered any chance to deploy and also have the crest clearance for the guns to fire. Major AK Kher captures and presents the difficulties faced in accomplishing this arduous task beautifully in the book. Ultimately it was accomplished to perfection by Major AK Kher and his Khalsa boys. It was a result of their sheer grit and determination. A slight mistake and the gun-carrying Kraz would have gone down in the Shyok river. I clearly remember standing at the bridge of Post 9 and looking up at the gun position in total disbelief.

The photographs of Rewari and Jaswant's post included in the book tell us the story of inadequacy of equipment and clothing of Indian troops during 1984—It is to the credit of Col AK Kher to remember and put in writing the events of 1985 in great detail. He has mentioned all those who were his comrades during difficult times. My unit carries very fond memories of 39 Medium, Major Kher and his men. Impetus was given to our operations all across the front on the southern glacier after arrival of 130 mm guns of 39 Medium at Post 9. We were hitting the enemy's rear at will, keeping his head always down. The biggest damage was caused to the enemy when Major AK Kher himself took to shooting from 'Yash' post. The total count on enemy side was one officer and 12 ORs killed and eight ORs seriously injured. This information was passed down to our battalion headquarters from Division Headquarters as a result of enemy radio intercepts. The radio intercepts also confirmed five enemy dead as a result of the shoot out carried out by Major Kher from 'Jaswant' post. Major AK Kher and 39 Medium had proved their professionalism and worth.

Being in command of a Khalsa Battery, his simple instructions to his men were always punctuated with the choicest of adjectives in Punjabi. The same style is reflected in this book too. I, as a youngster, was highly impressed with the respect Major AK Kher commanded from his troops. You earn respect from men if you genuinely care for them; Major Kher proved it amply.

As a souvenir, Major Kher had presented an empty shell to my unit on de-induction. It was converted into a beautiful lampshade which still finds pride of place in our Officers' Mess. Major Kher had given me a copy of the photograph of Turtuk which also finds a place in the book. It was converted into a painting when I was in command of my unit during our Silver Jubilee in 2001. I was lucky to go back to Turtuk as Commanding Officer of 18 Kumaon again, during 2002. To recollect the happenings of 1985, I once again stood at the bridge of Post 9, looked towards that flat patch where once Major Kher's guns were deployed. I could see only the traces of tracks leading to a flat patch which once took the guns up the hill against all odds in 1985. The area, once held by only my unit, was now the responsibility of four units. The memory of Major AK Kher, 39 Medium and their fire support to my unit 35 years ago is still fresh in my mind and will continue to linger on...

Col AK Kher has written this book in a language which everyone can understand, both civilians and people who don uniforms alike. The text of the book has been well supported with sketches and photographs which make it easy to understand the contents. Col Kher is an excellent photographer himself.

I enjoyed reading *Gunners at the Battlefront : Chhamb, Jelep La and Siachen* and I am sure anyone who holds even the slightest interest in military stories will cherish reading it. Col AK Kher has been ably supported by his son Ravi Kher in piecing together the events and present them in the shape which not only appeals to military personnel, but to a larger audience. I wish the book a great success.

Col VK Bahuguna, SM
18 Kumaon (Veteran)

(**Sena Medal Citation:** *Capt VK Bahuguna led a sensitive long-range patrol in high altitude area to assert our claim on the border. This involved traversing a distance of 150 kms of inhospitable terrain with areas prone to avalanches, glaciers, crevasses, steep cliffs and blizzards. The mission was accomplished despite immense exposure to risks. During the conduct of the mission, the patrol came across two anxious moments which would have resulted in certain death for some members and led to lowering of the morale of the whole team. But on both these occasions, Captain VK Bahuguna displayed great cool and courage and was instrumental in saving the lives of his team members with complete disregard to his own safety under extreme adverse and hostile conditions.)*

Infantry General's Perspective

It is a great pleasure for me to commend the efforts of my childhood friend, Ashok Kher. We both were in Kohima Company at OTS and began our army journey together. I had the privilege later in service to be the Colonel GS of the Division at Akhnoor which brought back memories of the area and the time spent there.

As Ralph Hawtrey aptly stated, "if war is an interruption between two periods of peace, it is equally true that peace is an interval between two wars." Mankind has been engaged in conflicts since its inception. In the last century or so, the world has fought two catastrophic wars: the First and the Second World War. Many thought that after the devastation of the Second World War, the world would see a long spell of peace. However, that was an illusion. Since the conclusion of the Second World War, the world has been beset with major internecine conflicts, highly offensive insurgencies, communal conflicts, colossal human migration, oil wars, ethnic cleansing actions and terrorist networks spread over the entire globe.

Obviously man does not learn from history. Had that been true, mankind would have been treading a different terrain today. Colonel Kher's excursion into our military past brings out vividly the treacherous terrain of adversarial plans to weaken India. Swinging between our northern borders in Jammu & Kashmir to northeast India during his service tour,

Colonel Kher has had a rewarding career during which he got the unique opportunity to serve the entire spectrum of our borders along our two fierce adversaries, Pakistan and China. The account of his service and many battles and tribulations alongwith the rich experiences of his travels within China has lent a deep and refreshing perspective to his account.

Colonel Kher's account of the Pakistani assault in Chhamb-Jaurian sector in December 1971 would impel any military mind to evaluate the dangers inherent in a strategy of consistency. The Indian side adopted a defensive posture in this sector and was sanguine in its decision to halt the enemy in its tracks should it have ventured to attempt an offensive through this sector. How churlish could such thinking be? Our troops and defences faced a heavy and devastating onslaught from the enemy in this sector as a result of a totally ill-considered and flawed defensive posture.

If consistency of defence in war with total mental inertia would be a hobgoblin of big minds, armies would have no trouble in escaping the demon. Should we, the military men, forget what Marshal Foch said in the First World War when asked about his status in the midst of an attack: "My centre is giving way, my right is retreating, situation excellent, I am attacking." And again the legendary Gen Douglas Mac Arthur's bold plan of Inchon landings in Korea turned the tide of communist onslaught and saved the Korean peninsula when the entire American General's staff had opposed Mac Arthur's invasion plan. Georgy Zukhov in Stalingrad and Gen Giap in the Battle of Dien Bien Phu are classic examples of boldness and foresight in war. Colonel Kher advises that strategy, based on taking into account all facets of the situation on hand and the tools and tactics to translate that strategy into victory on ground, should be soundly formulated with boldness and focus.

Colonel Kher's tour in the Siachen Glacier, where he was among the first pioneer to set up a post, is most informative and revealing. Colonel Kher displays considerable strategic understanding and suggests the wastefulness of this unnecessary but complicated posture. However, this may not be entirely advisable in India's immediate neighbourhood which is fraught with suspicion and territorial ambition. This reminds one of the French statesmen Tallyrand, who said: "War is far too serious a business to be left to Generals." Probably political and geo-strategic compulsions abounding in our nation warrant a forward and bold posture on Siachen. Siachen is the future water source of the Indian sub-continent. It is also an essential sentinel post for an unpredictable adversary China, who, in cohorts with Pakistan, is out to create trouble. One may also heed the sage advice of the architect of modern India, Pandit Jawaharlal Nehru, who in the run up to India's Independence in 1947, said that it was not a mile of territory that mattered; it was the integrity and the character of a nation that mattered in retaining that mile of territory.

Gunners at the Battlefront : Chhamb, Jelep La and Siachen is a career-biography of a soldier, who has tried to piece together his passion for the nation while serving it with such dedication and fervour for over 30 years and while doing so, he narrates, for the fellow citizens, the sacrifices, triumphs and tribulations that a service career gives one. He has told the story succinctly and sincerely. It is a story that would stand us in good stead if we take heed of it and learn from it. The book is written in a typical military style, forthright and straightforward. I recommend this book to practitioners of the military profession and civilians alike, for better understanding of the art of war.

Mumbai
28th May, 2020

—Maj Gen TK Kaul,
PVSM, AVSM, VSM
(Veteran)

Artillery General Recalls

I was commissioned in June 1963; thereafter, I served in five Artillery Regiments. I joined 39 Medium Regiment in mid June 1971. It was at (Chakki Bank) Pathankot that I took over command of 122 Medium Battery. The Regiment was part of 10 Artillery Brigade and that was the time when Captain Ashok Kumar Kher was in 127 Division Locating Battery.

In September 1971, 39 Medium Regiment moved to Kathua (Jammu & Kashmir) for an annual training camp. In the beginning of October 1971, the unit was asked to move to 10 Infantry Division from the training area. The unit, on arrival in Division sector, was moved to a concentration area and then to a temporary gun area before participating in the war from there till the fall of the western bank of Mannawar Tawi.

Meanwhile, Ashok was moved to headquarter 10 Artillery Brigade, as I learnt later. Therefore Ashok had the advantage of seeing the whole division sector while surveying the complete area and establishing the theatre grid for the guns. Thereafter he was in FDC with Brigade Major Artillery assisting him there. Therefore, he was aware of the complete situation of the operations taking place in the 10 Division sector on a day-to-day basis during the war.

On 14th/15th December, the unit was moved to 80 Infantry Brigade ex-25 Infantry Division to support an offensive there which was however later abandoned due to the implementation of ceasefire with effect from the midnight of 16/17 December.

My association with him was very limited and mainly after the ceasefire, when the unit returned to Akhnoor in 10 Division Sector by the end of December, 1971 and he was posted to the unit from the headquarter Artillery Brigade.

The unit thereafter moved to 25 Infantry Division Sector in mid 1972 and remained there till the end of February 1973 before moving to 33 Corps Zone in March 1973. On arrival, the unit was deployed in parts: Regimental HQ with 122 Medium Battery at Ridge area near 17 Milestone insp. of 17 Mountain Division; 123 Medium Battery in 27 Mountain Division Sector in Woodcock area and 393 Medium Battery remained at Sukhna with HQ 33 Corps Artillery Brigade.

My stay in Sikkim was very short as I was posted out to a peace station.

Thereafter I met Ashok in May 1985, at Basoli when I took over the command of 39 Medium Regiment. 122 Medium Battery, which Ashok was commanding, moved to 102 Infantry Brigade sector (Siachen Glacier) with a troop of guns which he assembled and deployed at Post 9 and he took over the troop at Base Camp, that is, the Siachen area in mid June 1985.

In July 1985, I visited the Battery at Base Camp area and then in September or so visited Turtuk valley area where a troop of the battery was moved and deployed. Ashok's efforts with the battery on the glacier were commended by GOC 3 Infantry Division and the commanders of 102 Infantry Brigade and 3 Artillery Brigade through their DOs.

By the end of November 1985, the unit moved to Alwar prior to our departure from Basoli, when 122 Medium Battery had rejoined the unit. Alwar again was a very short stay for me, i.e. December 1985 to April 1986. I handed over the command of the unit to the late Col RP Sharma in the third week of April 1986 in Delhi Field Firing Range and came to Alwar, did the packing and moved in beginning of May to Tactical Wing School of Artillery as DS.

Though it is almost 50 years ago that all the events took place, most of us may be having foggy ideas about these happenings, but not Ashok.

He has a very vivid memory about these happenings and has described them in his very own style, almost ad verbatim. I am very sure that the reader will get a very good idea of our unit's achievements and youngsters of the unit will get to know these events.

My heartiest congratulations to Ashok for this tremendous work and wish him all the best for times to come...

Thank you and Jai Hind!

—Maj Gen JRK Bhattacharji
(Veteran)

(Col JRK Bhattacharji went to S of A as DS in Tac Wg. In May 1990 he moved on, getting promoted as Brigadier to command 6 Mtn Arty Bde at Raiwala near Haridwar. He was there till February 1993 and then moved to AHQ as Dy MS-11(Arty).

Then on promotion as Maj Gen, he took over ADG CAB (Complaints and Advisory Board) to COAS in September, 1995 and had the privilege to serve with Gen Shanker Roy Choudhary for two years and later with Gen VP Malik for three-and-a-half months till mid January, 1998. He went on to serve as MG Arty HQ, Southern Command till November 1999. Thereafter, as Deputy Commandant, School of Arty from December 1999 to April 2001. Maj Gen JRK Bhattacharji hung up his boots on 31st March, 2002 as MG Arty HQ Central Command.)

Introduction

I passed out of SSC (non-technical) course 5, Officers Training School, Madras on 22nd June, 1968. The Passing-Out-Parade salute was taken by Lt General Harbakhsh Singh, VrC. He was a war hero and General Officer Commanding-in-Chief, Western Command.

Upon passing out, I joined 127 Division Locating Battery at Amritsar, Punjab as a young Second Lieutenant and after 32 years of military service, finally took voluntary retirement as a Lieutenant Colonel in the year 2000.

There are several accounts of the battle of Chhamb that took place in the 1971 war between India and Pakistan and so this certainly is not a new subject to write about.

When one undergoes something as intense and metamorphic as a battle, it leaves a certain imprint on one's mind which seldom allows one to forget the events that transpired.

What necessitated me to write this book is to present a young Captain's view of the battle. As such, every incident described in this book is crystal clear in my mind as if it's happening right now.

At the onset, I would like to declare that views/events are those witnessed by me or received as first-hand information during the war and are in no way meant to harm anyone in whatsoever fashion. Most of the people mentioned in this book are either known to me or are people with whom I interacted during the course of my intensive artillery survey work prior to the start of the battle.

Moreover, due to my pre-war ground survey work, I had intimate knowledge of the terrain and deployment in the 10 Infantry Division sector.

On 3rd December, 1971, I was present in the nerve centre at the Artillery Fire Direction Centre (FDC), right in between the forward defended and depth localities of 5 Sikh Regiment, very close to CFL. Here one had the actual ground picture of the happenings on every battalion front during the war in the Chhamb sector.

It was a Pakistani division plus strength assault on Chhamb with Indian 191 Infantry Brigade and one unit of 28 Infantry Brigade facing the full brunt of it. The enemy fired a heavy concentration of artillery on our BOPs and defences, totally pulverising us. Maximum casualties were inflicted on us by accurate and heavy volumes of artillery fire.

Our Artillery Regiments deployed for offensive action were only engaging in defensive fire tasks. When the enemy formed up for attack, we fired concentrations of artillery salvos to disrupt the attacks. All guns were continuously firing, with no maintenance and rest.

There was so much demand for defensive artillery fire to prevent the enemy from overrunning our posts that on a few occasions, at the same time, a battery was given two targets to engage on at a 100 degree arc variance. There was also a desperate occasion when only a single medium gun was allocated to an OP Officer to engage the targets as there was not enough battery/troop strength to cover all arcs against the enemy onslaught.

The initial years of my military career, from 1968 to 1971, were with 127 Div. Loc Battery and from 1971 to 1974, during and immediately after the war, I spent my life with 39 Medium Regiment, solidifying my bond with the men.

In 1974, I got posted out from 39 Medium Regiment in Sikkim to 126 Div. Loc Battery in Darangdra, Gujarat. I further spent a number of years with other units and locations until 1982. I had a homecoming of sorts as I got posted back to 39 Medium Regiment as a Battery Commander in Basoli Camp, Jammu.

In 1985, with 39 Medium Regiment, I had the honour to serve the country under Operation Meghdoot at Siachen, the highest battlefield in the world. The description in this book is of my own actions and without mentioning the stories of the magnificent men under my command, the narration would have been incomplete.

Ever since I hung up my boots in the year 2000, there has not been a single day that I have not thought about my men and the time that we endured in war and peace. This book is dedicated to the memories that I have of them and how they lifted me.

A soldier never quits and I think every true soldier wants to die in uniform. The allure of the uniform is such that if called upon in war, I am willing to serve at the age of 71 with my Unit 39 Medium Regiment.

This book is an ode to my Unit 39 Medium Regiment and the real valour that I have witnessed on ground with my men and a lot of it remains unsung and unknown. A lot of my men and comrades have passed on without the world even knowing about them. This book is an attempt to show respect and regard for the families of the departed souls. Instead of mundane dinner conversations reminiscing about my time with them, I strive, through this book, to praise their valour and determination.

I must thank my son Ravi who forced me to narrate while he painstakingly wrote every sentence, fact checking where necessary and refining the flow to make it into a more presentable account.

I am immensely proud of and grateful to my wife Renu, who walked reassuringly by my side in all my duties, including that of Commanding Officer.

The things that have taken place between India and Pakistan since 1949 now seem beyond the comprehension of a regular Army officer. Why did we lose territory in Chhamb in 1971 when the enemy had already demonstrated their ability in 1965? Why didn't we plug the gaps? Why didn't we counterattack and why does Pakistan still have Indian POWs while we released 90,000 of theirs? Why did we create Bangladesh and leave Jammu & Kashmir unresolved?

India is spending crores of rupees per day since 1984 on Siachen to fight on a wasteland where nature is the biggest enemy, successfully killing us.

These are the few questions that haunt me even today and I am grappling to find the answers to them.

A few years ago, during my travel to Hong Kong, I met an American commercial pilot. Upon finding out that I was an Indian Army veteran, he immediately said, "Thank you for your service." I found the Americans very naturally respecting people from the Armed Forces, not necessarily their own, whereas the Indian Prime Minister had to appeal to the general public to applaud the Armed Forces in India.

On my extensive travels in China, in 2018, I was pleasantly surprised to see the country's progress reaching its full potential as a leading world economy and a powerhouse–a far cry from the cheap PLA uniforms I noticed in 1973 while being posted on the China border. My first bullet-train ride was in China, from Shanghai to the industrial city of Tang Shan, near Beijing.

I had the opportunity to inspect one of the biggest steel plants with impressive technology and cutting-edge machinery. I recall being amazed at the infrastructure and the country's progressive outlook. The Chinese cities that I visited were spotlessly clean and the general population disciplined and respectful.

In the end, no soldier wants war but he has to be prepared for one. The future wars will be technology-driven and the Indian Army has to upgrade and be prepared. The Indian soldier stock is by far the best in terms of physical capability and character as he can perform in any terrain with minimal facilities and tools. I admit though that the training has to evolve with increased technology and artificial intelligence.

War is no longer limited to land, sea and air.

—Lt Col AK Kher
(Veteran)

Acknowledgement

Special thanks are due to Mayur Keny for the Maps and Swapna Mishra for the Cover design and for their wholehearted support.

Contents

VOLUME I

BATTLE
OF
CHHAMB, 1971

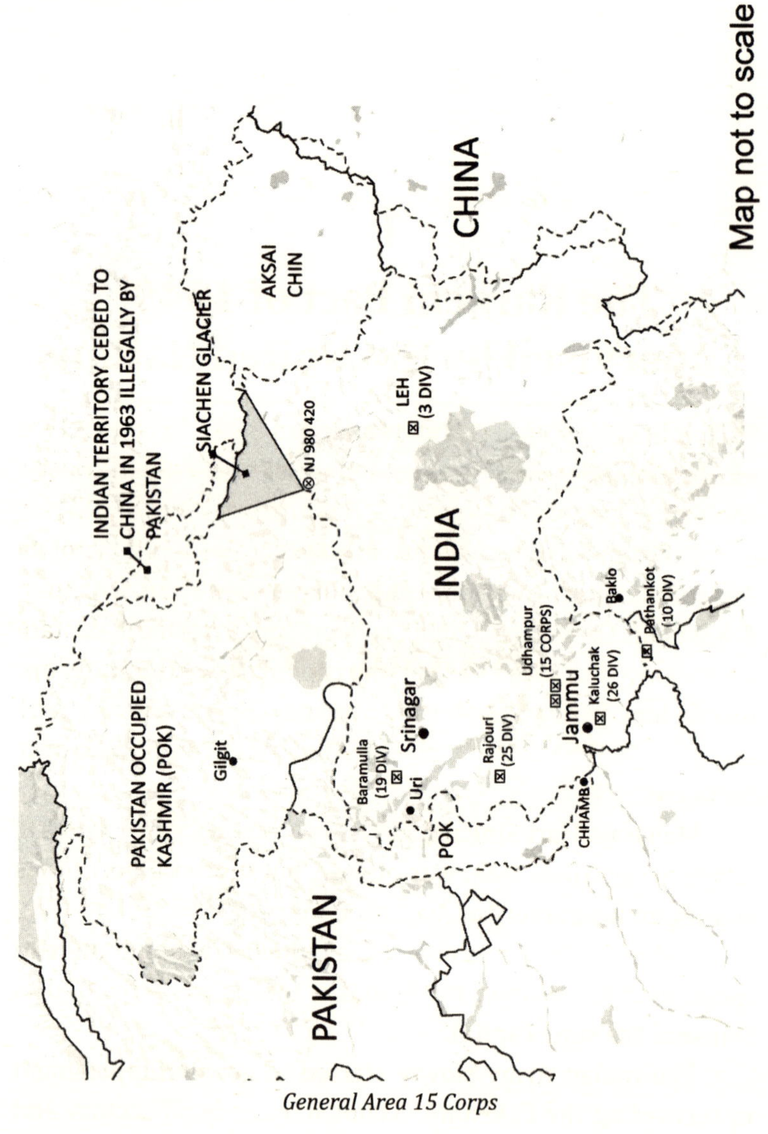

General Area 15 Corps

1

The Karachi Pact of 1949, Supervised by the United Nations

The first Kashmir war broke out in 1947 between two newly independent nations, India and Pakistan over the princely state of Jammu & Kashmir.

Pakistan launched its tribal Lashkar on 22nd October, 1947 in an effort to capture the independent state of Jammu & Kashmir. These local tribal Lashkars and irregular Pakistani forces moved to take Srinagar, the capital city of the state; but on reaching Baramulla, short of Srinagar, they resorted to rape and plunder. They were stalled in their objective to take over Srinagar.

Maharaja Hari Singh made a plea to India for assistance, out of desperation. Help was offered, but it was subject to his signing an Instrument of Accession to India.

Following the accession of the Jammu & Kashmir state to India on 26th October, 1947, Indian troops were airlifted to Srinagar, the state capital.

The Indian Army slowly started to get the upper hand in recovering the Pakistani-occupied areas in all sectors and while the military operations were ongoing, India took the matter to the UN Security Council, which passed Resolution 39 (1948) and established the United Nations Commission for India and Pakistan (UNCIP) to investigate the issues and mediate between the two countries.

After intense negotiations, a formal ceasefire was declared on the night of 31st December, 1948 after nearly a year of fighting and became effective on the night of 1st January, 1949.

The ceasefire, after the hostilities, came to be known as the Cease-Fire Line (CFL).

The UN also established the United Nations Military Observer Group in India and Pakistan (UNMOGIP) to monitor the ceasefire line; this monitoring lasted till December, 1971.

Following the above UN intervention, the Karachi Pact was signed on 27th July, 1949 by the military representatives Lt Gen SM Shrinagesh on behalf of India, Maj Gen WJ Cawthorn on behalf of Pakistan and Hernando Samper and Lt Gen M Delvoie from UNCIP.

This agreement restricted deployment of troops only to a Corps level strength in Jammu & Kashmir.

The XV Corps also know as the Chinar Corps, Head Quarter (HQ) was stationed at Udhampur of which:

(a) 3 Infantry Division was located at Leh to guard the border with Pakistan from Nubra Valley to Sonamarg and the border with China at Karakorum.

(b) 19 Infantry Division was located at Baramulla to guard Sonamarg, Gurrez, Uri and from Kishan Ganga valley up to Haji Peer.

(c) 25 Infantry Division was located at Rajouri to guard Peer Panchal, Poonch, Rajouri, and Naushera.

(d) 26 Infantry Division was located at Kaluchak for guarding Jammu-Samba region.

(e) 10 Infantry Division was located at Pathankot and was tasked to guard from Akhnoor to Kalidhar Ridge. In this area, the ceasefire line (CFL) ran from west to east, from Nowshera upto Kalidhar Ridge

> and turned southwest to enter the plains opposite Dewa and ended near Mannawar and from Sangam, the international border, ran eastwards towards Pathankot.

Due to limitations imposed by the Karachi Pact, not all assets of 10 Infantry Division could be located in Jammu & Kashmir.

UN Observer Group

The UN Commission for India and Pakistan monitored the deployment, location and positions of troops on the ground on a regular basis under the Karachi Pact. Any movement or new diggings, etc. were regularly reported by the Commission as violations on both sides of the ceasefire line (CFL).

The UN observer group comprised mainly of officers and men from New Zealand and the Canadian Army. They were always neutral in their approach.

The UN monitoring did not stop the two countries from going to war repeatedly. India and Pakistan went to War in 1965 ,1971 and 1999.

□

*For the purpose of Volume I, the focus is on operational conduct of 10 Infantry Division in 1971 only.

2

Initial Plan of 10 Infantry Division in Defence of Chhamb Jaurian before 1st November, 1971

The Border Observation Posts (BOPs) all along the Ceasefire Line (CFL) and International Boundary (IB) were guarded by two Battalions—51 and 57 of the Border Security Force (BSF).

The BOPs were as under: Picket 707, Laleali, Red Hill, New Green, Pir Jamal, Moel, Paur, Bokan, Dalla, Burejal, Bhusa and Mannawar on or very close to the Ceasefire Line. Across Mannawar Tawi—From Sangam to Akhnoor was the International Boundary.

The Defensive Positions of 10 Infantry Division were as follows: HQ 10 Infantry Division was at Pathankot, Punjab outside of Jammu & Kashmir.

HQ 10 Artillery Brigade was stationed at Pathankot of which only:

- One Artillery Regiment, 18 Field and 127 Division Locating Battery (Div. Loc) were stationed at Jaurian, Jammu & Kashmir in 191 Infantry Brigade sector.
- One Artillery Battery of 12 Field Regiment was deployed permanently in 28 Infantry Brigade sector at Katau, Jammu & Kashmir.

Rest all the other elements of the Artillery Brigade were stationed in Pathankot itself, out of J & K.

One Armoured Regiment 9 Deccan Horse was located at Pavan Di Chack (PDC).

52 Infantry Brigade was stationed at Baklo, Dharamshala outside of Jammu & Kashmir due to limitations imposed by the Karachi Pact.

28 Infantry Brigade was deployed in hilly areas of Sundarbani, guarding Kalidhar Ridge in Jammu & Kashmir.

191 Infantry Brigade was the only Infantry Brigade deployed for guarding areas from Chhamb, Jaurian to Akhnoor in Jammu & Kashmir.

Elements of 191 Infantry Brigade deployed in positions as below:

5 Sikh covering Chhamb and their defences extending along Gopar, Phagla Ridge, Pt 994, Sakrana and Mandiala.

5 Assam along Troti heights with defences extending till Khore-Lam area.

4/1 Gorkha was deployed defending Dhon Chak along Troti Heights.

127 Division Locating Battery was to deploy a long sound-ranging base along Lokhi Khad and Khore area.

Upon commencement of Pakistani attack, the units in location of 191 Infantry Brigade were tasked to defend the two approaches to Akhnoor as follows:

(a) Northern Approach: The Northern Axis was an unmetalled, gravelled track, starting from Sukhtau Nullah via Mandiala crossing, Bucho Mandi, Kachrial, Chaprial, Kalith, Pahari Wala, PDC, Fatowal Ridge and reaching Akhnoor. It is also known as old Akhnoor Road.

The PAPA Force comprised of 5 Sikh and one squadron of Deccan Horse to fight successive delaying battles, protecting the northern approach till Troti Heights and subsequently deployed in depth at Kalith in main defences.

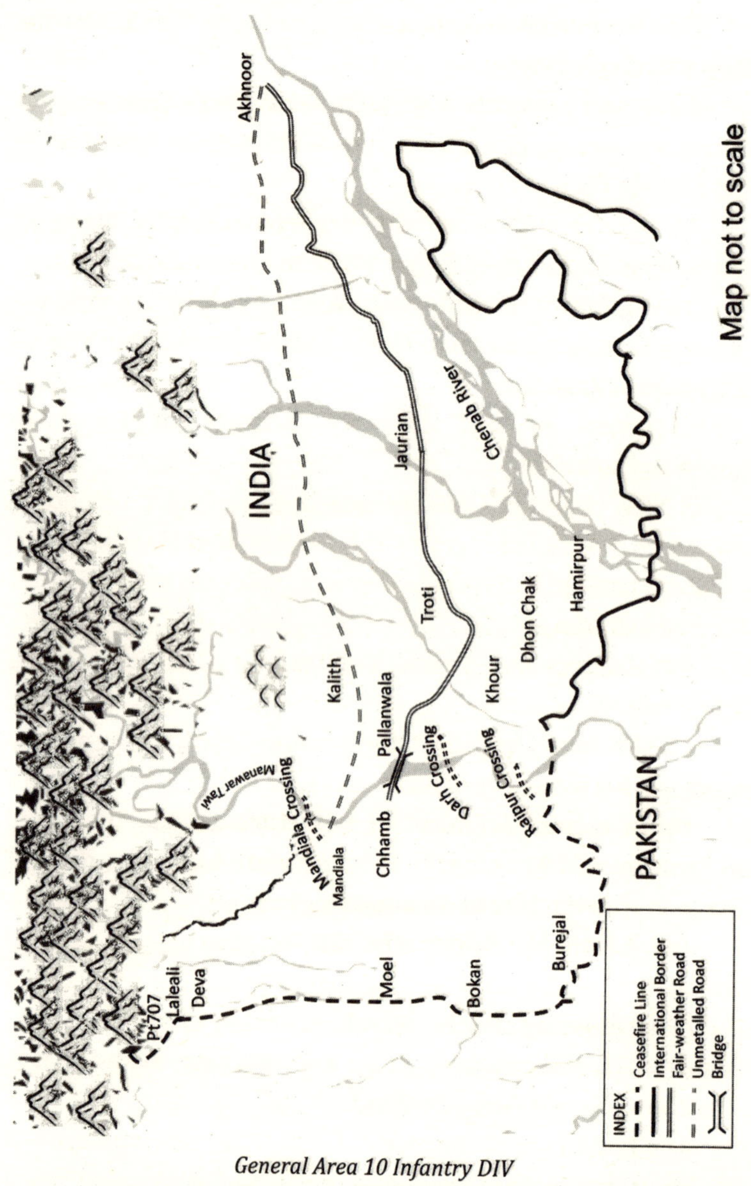

General Area 10 Infantry DIV

(b) The Southern Approach: The Southern Axis was the main metalled road connecting Chhamb to Akhnoor; starting from Chhamb Bridge, through Pallanwala, Khore, Dhol Forest, Jaurian, Fatowal Ridge and reaching Akhnoor.

The QUEBEC Force comprised of two companies, 4/1 Gorkha and one squadron of Deccan Horse to deploy forward and fight successive delaying battles with the enemy along the southern approach till Troti heights.

Additionally 5 Assam was to provide defences from Khore Area, Dhon Chak, Lam to Hamirpur, covering the Southern Axis.

18 Field Artillery Regiment was to give direct supporting fire to forward units and fight delaying battle from various temporary positions in Pallanwala and finally deploy in main defences around Troti Heights.

After blunting and holding Pakistani attacks in the Kalith area, Troti heights and Dhon Chak, a massive counterattack by fresh elements of 10 Infantry Division and ex Corps reserves would throw back the Pakistanis from the area. The Chhamb salient was bisected by Mannawar Tawi and was connected with one proper all-weather Chhamb Bridge and three fords used for dry weather crossing they being Mandiala, Darh and Raipur crossings connecting defences in the east to those in the west over Mannawar Tawi and making a total of four crossings.

Defences in depth at Kalith – Troti – Dhon Chak were very well prepared and practiced.

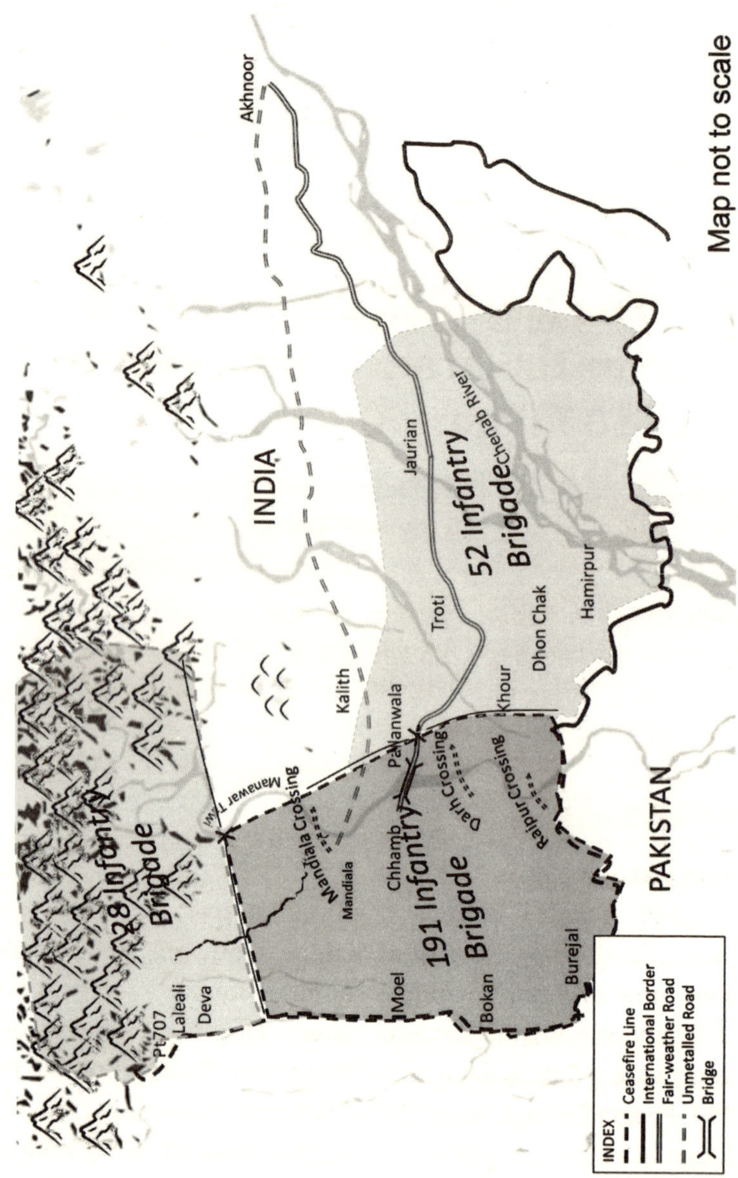

Infantry Brigade Locations in 10 Infantry DIV Area

3

The Modified Defence Plan after the Army Chief's Visit to 10 Infantry Division Area

The Army Chief, General Sam Manekshaw came to 10 Infantry Division area on 1st November, 1971. He addressed all officers at the Bhyram Club, Rukhmuthi, delivering his famous speech, "When you are in Pakistan, hands in pockets and keep advancing."

'The territory west of Mannawar Tawi to be defended and our territorial integrity to be fully maintained' was the Chief's order, which was contrary to the delaying battle plans of 10 Infantry Division.

New Attack Plans

191 Infantry Brigade deployed at well-practiced and prepared defensive areas of Kalith, Troti and Dhon Chak were now ordered to completely move forward across west of Mannawar Tawi to Chhamb salient. They were now tasked to provide a firm base in areas Mannawar, Jhanda, Burejal, Pt 994, Phagla Ridge, Ghopar Ridge, Sakrana Ridge and Mandiala Ridge area for an attack on Pakistan, instead of fighting a delaying battle in Kalith – Troti – Dhon Chak area.

An additional force comprised of the Alpha group 9 Para SF and ex Corps reserves 68 Infantry Brigade, 216 Medium

Regiment and 72 Armoured Regiment (newly raised in Ahmednagar, just a few months ago) moved into location at Akhnoor – Jaurian – Troti area of 10 Infantry Division sector for carrying out the strike.

68 Infantry Brigade was concentrated in Akhnoor area and was tasked to attack all Border Outpost (BOPs) of Pakistan in advance. Additionally they were also to capture the ditch-cum-bund system obstacle defences set up by the Pakistani Army.

52 Infantry Brigade was also ordered to move in from Baklo, Dharamshala and occupy some of the 191 Infantry Brigade-vacated defensive sectors alongside Chatti Tali, Thako Chak, 15 Alpha and Molu sector. This sector had major obstacles, like the Chenab river and the delta of Mannawar Tawi, making these areas generally marshy and unsuitable for a Pakistani armoured thrust.

All elements of 10 Artillery Brigade from Pathankot and ex Corps reserve (216 Medium Regiment from Chandi Mandir) also arrived and deployed in their operational locations in Chhamb. The Field Artillery Regiments were now deployed in forward locations across west of Mannawar Tawi and closer to the ceasefire line. The Medium Regiments were deployed on the east banks on the home-side of Mannawar Tawi to enable hitting in-depth Pakistani defensive locations, to support the attack by 68 Infantry Brigade along with 72 Armour Regiment. If questioned by UN observers, upon sightings of such large numbers of troops and guns, directions were to tell them that 10 Infantry Division was on an exercise and would be returning soon.

The Order of Battle

15 Corps was commanded by Lt Gen Sartaj Singh

10 Infantry Division

The Division Commander was GOC Major General Jaswant Singh, VSM.

Col General Staff (GS) was Col Shankar Lala Rege, ADMS was Col White.

10 Infantry Div. consisted of the following brigades:

28 Infantry Brigade

Commanded by Brigadier Russi Bajina (VrC), it comprised the following units:

- 8 J & K Militia, commanded by Lt Col Randhawa who was from Gorkha battalion.
- 2 JAK Rifles, commanded by Lt Col Gill; the Adjutant was Major Matta.
- 5 Rajput, commanded by Lt Col Sarfaraz.

191 Infantry Brigade

Commanded by Brigadier RK Jasbir Singh who was replaced by an Armored Corps officer, Brigadier Satish Mathur. The process of handing and take over was on going when the war broke out. This meant that during the battle there were two Brigadiers in HQ 191 Infantry Brigade. 191 Infantry Brigade comprised of the following units:

- 5 Sikh, commanded by Lt Col PK Khanna, 2IC Major BL Malhotra.
- 5 Assam, commanded by Lt Col AS Malhi; Adjutant was Captain SR Dass.
- 4/1 Gorkha, commanded by Lt Col Bawal.
- 10 Garhwal, commanded by Lt Col Onkar Singh (This Battalion disposition was in general area of 52 Infantry Brigade.)

52 Infantry Brigade

Commanded by Brigadier KK Hazara it comprised the following units:

- 7 Garhwal, commanded by Lt Col JB Rana
- 16 Punjab, commanded by Lt Col Raghubir Singh
- 3/4 Gorkha

68 Infantry Brigade (Ex-Corp Reserve)

Commanded by Brigadier Trevor Morlin and it comprised of the following units:

- 7 Kumaon, commanded by Lt Col Dahiya.
- 9 JAT, commanded by Lt Col Jagjit Singh.
- 5/8 Gorkha, commanded by Lt Col AS Kalkat.

9 Para SF was commanded by Lt Col OP Sabharwal. **Alpha Group** Commanded by Major Ashok Cariappa was deployed in 10 Infantry Div. sector.

10 Artillery Brigade

Commanded by Brigadier K Srinivasan, a very tough commander, known as Henry.

The Brigade Major (BM) was Major Surya Narayan, the DQ was Major Baldev Raj, EME Artillery was Major Sekho, the G3 was Captain Bali, the IO was Captain Passi, the Staff Captain Q was Captain Puri, the ACBO were Captain Anil Khanna and Captain Akhilesh, the Sparrow was Lt PK Sharma, the Survey Troop Commander was Captain AK Kher and the Education Officer was Lt Daulat Ram.

10 Artillery Brigade had the following units:

- 12 Field Regiment commanded by Lt Col AB Guha and Adjutant was Captain Roberts.
- 18 Field Regiment commanded by Lt Col Verma. The Adjutant was Captain Dev.

- 81 Field Regiment commanded by Lt Col Vinod Uppal. The Adjutant was Captain Manmohan Singh.
- 39 Medium Regiment commanded by Lt Col BC Gauri Shankar. Adjutant was Captain Prakash Pande.
- Ex Corps reserves was 216 Medium Regiment, commanded by Lt Col ML Sethi. The Adjutant was Captain Mahajini.
- 1512 AD Battery commanded by Major KN Khanna of 151 Air Defence Regiment.
- One Troop of L60 commanded by Captain Kaul of 45 Air Defence Regiment.
- 1 Anti Tank Guided Missile (ATGM) Platoon of 12 Guards - Jonga based, commanded by Captain K Puri who was the son of movie actor, Madan Puri.
- 127 Division Locating Battery was commanded by Major Sohal. The 2IC was Captain BS Sandhu, Captain UC Shrivastava was radar section commander and Captain AK Kher was part of this Battery deputed to 10 Artillery Brigade HQ.

Captain Padmanabhan and Captain Dillon of the Air Observation Post,piloted 2 unarmed and slow moving Krishak Aircraft. They operated from Rukhmuthi Advance Landing Ground (ALG).

During the war the ALG at Khore was constructed by the survey troop boys of Captain AK Kher.

Both the Air Observation officers were not able to identify suitable targets for engagement due to lack of visibility and fog of war. Captain AK Kher was tasked by Brigadier Srinivasan to fly and observe enemy positions with both Air OPs prior to and during war. Captain Padmanabhan flew a lot of observation missions along with Captain AK Kher. Subsequently Captain Dillon was deputed to another sector.

Armoured Regiments

9 Deccan Horse of T54 tanks was commanded by Lt Col AS Bal, 2IC Major HN Hoon. The Adjutant was Captain Surendra Kaushik.

Ex. Corp's Reserve was 72 Armoured Regiment of T55 tanks commanded by Lt Col Inderjit Chopra.

Signals

10 Infantry Division Signal Regiment commanded by Lt Col V Balachandran. The 2IC was Major RS Anand.

68 Infantry Brigade Signal Company (Ex-Corp Reserves)

Engineer Regiments

- 61 Engineer Regiment
- 106 Engineer Regiment

□

4

Deployment of 10 Infantry Division on Ground for Attack

(A) 28 Infantry Brigade deployed for the defence of Kalidhar Ridge and Sundarbani area.

(i) Initially 5 Rajput Battalion was deployed on Sundarbani heights. Just before the war broke out, they moved to areas like Nathuan Tibba and adjacent hills.

(ii) 2 JAK Rifles was deployed on Kalidhar Ridge and Katau area. This was a mountainous region that did not allow any large-scale operations.

(iii) 8 J & K Militia, was deployed as follows:

1. One company commanded by Major Sharma at Pt 707.
2. One company commanded by Major Virendra Kumar Sahi at Laleali.
3. One company commanded by Captain Mandal at Dewa.
4. One company commanded by Major Bhasin at Nathuan Tibba (Artillery Range Area)

It is to be noted that the J & K Militia was not a regular army battalion but an old J & K force battalion commanded by regular Indian Army officers. Their salaries, pensions and other entitlements were lower than the Indian Army. However, they fought most valiantly in this war and yielded very little ground against heavy enemy attacks.

(B) 191 Infantry Brigade deployed to provide firm base in Chhamb area, covering ceasefire line (CFL) from Dewa to Mannawar post.

(i) 5 Sikh was deployed to cover Pt 994 (303 mtr grid map), Phagla, Gurha and Mandiala Heights.

1. One company was deployed at Pt 994 commanded by Major DS Pannu.
2. One company was deployed at Phagla Ridge commanded by Major Jaivir Singh. Captain Khanna was part of it.
3. One company deployed in depth on Sakrana Ridge commanded by Major BL Malhotra along with Battalion HQ.
4. One company was commanded by Major Ram Chandran at Mandiala heights guarding Chhamb Bridge and Sukhtau Nullah. Captain Siddhu was part of the company.

(ii) 5 Assam was deployed in area Burejal, Dalla, Bokan, Pt 951, Gogi, Barsala and Singri.

1. One company at Pt 951 commanded Major PK Puri.
2. One company at Gogi Barsala commanded by Major JBS Makin.
3. 2 companies in depth at Singri along with battalion HQ, one of which was commanded by Major Mukhtiar Singh Sehrawat. A platoon of Major Mukhtiar's company was deployed forward.

(iii) 4/1 Gorkha was deployed from area Chak Pandit, Mannawar, Malkay camp, Mangotia, Jhanda and Bhusa.

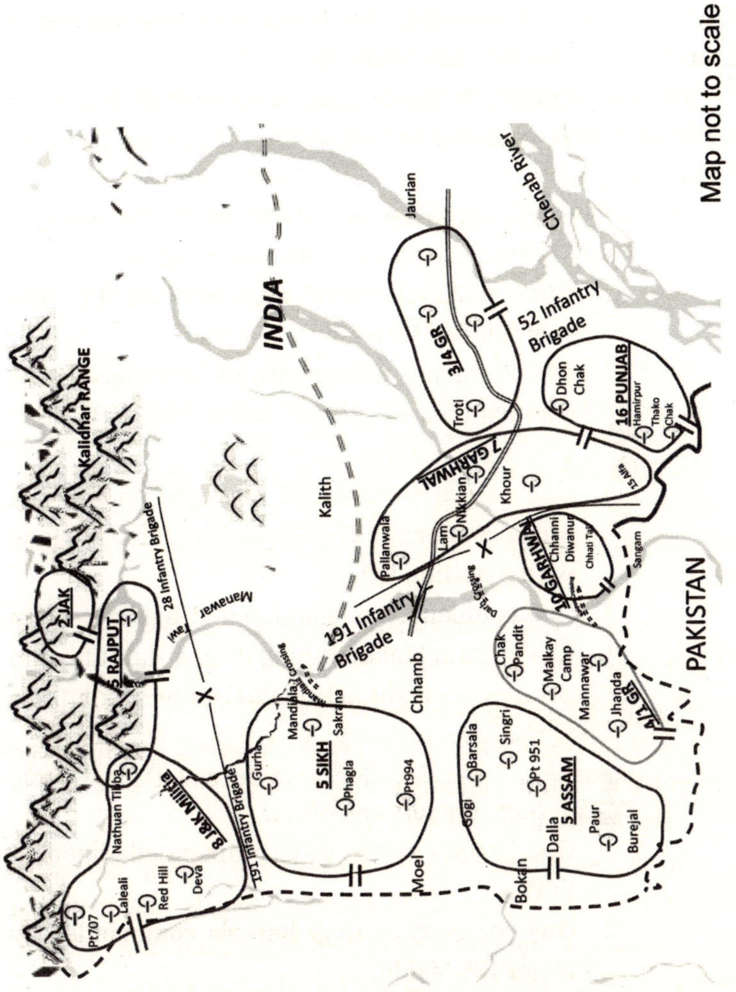

Deployment of Infantry Battallions in 10 Div. Area

1. One company at Mannawar post was commanded by Major DP Lakhanpal.
2. One Company at Jhanda was commanded by Major Rajinder Singh, with a section under Lieutenant Khati at Mangotia.
3. One company in depth at Malkay camp.

4. One company in depth was commanded by Major Gian Singh at Chak Pandit along with battalion HQ.

(iv) 10 Garhwal was deployed east of the river in areas Raipur Crossing, Chatti Tali, Garadh and Gigrial.

(C) 52 Infantry Brigade was guarding the international boundary.

(i) 16 Punjab was deployed in areas of 15 Alpha, Thako Chak, Sainth and Garadh.

(ii) 7 Garhwal was deployed in Pallanwala covering Lam, Nikkiar, Khore village area along Tawi banks and basic area opposite Chatti Tali. The Company commanders were Major Bhandari, Major Sherawat and Captain Saini.

(iii) 3/4 Gorkha was deployed in depth areas protecting the Akhnoor Road.

The area from Sangam to Molu was at the confluence of Chenab and Mannawar Tawi with vast stretches of waterlogged areas on both sides of the IB. This rendered the area unsuitable for armoured thrust. However, Pakistan used armour with limited effect in this area.

(D) Deployment of Alfa Group SF

In 4 team formations headed by Captain Macarius, Captain Cariappa, Captain AS Bist and Captain KC Padha at, the junction of Sukhtau Nallah and Mannawar Tawi close to Chhamb Bridge and in vicinity of 216 Medium forward Battery.

(E) 10 Artillery Brigade deployed as under:

(i) 12 Field Regiment.

1. One Battery was deployed in Sundarbani-Katau area in 28 Infantry Brigade area.
2. Two Batteries across Mannawar Tawi, general area Sakrana.

(ii) 81 Field Regiment.

All 3 Batteries in area Sakrana across the Chhamb bridge in the vicinity of 12 Field Regiment

(iii) 18 Field Regiment.

1. One Battery in area Sakrana across Chhamb Bridge commanded by Captain Sukhwant Singh Gill.
2. Two Batteries deployed in area Nikkiar on the home side of the river in 52 Infantry Brigade Area.

(iv) 86 Light Regiment.

1. One Battery was deployed in Sundarbani in 28 Infantry Brigade sector covering Kalidhar ridge.
2. One Battery was deployed in Kheri which was near Dewa closer to CFL, commanded by Major Gurdav.
3. One Battery (Congo Battery) was deployed in area Akhnoor, commanded by Major Khara.

(v) 39 Medium Regiment.

All 3 Batteries were deployed alongside a *nullah* near Kachrial Chaprial heights away from the banks of Mannawar Tawi. Major Ranbir was in command of 393 Medium Battery. He was with 9 Para SF. Major JRK Bhattacharji was in command of 122 Medium Battery. He was with 52 Infantry Brigade HQ and Major Dhinsa was in command of 123 Medium Battery and was available in gun area.

(vi) 216 Medium Regiment (ex Corps Reserve)

All batteries were deployed towards north of 39 Medium Regiment near Kachrial Chaprial heights much closer to the banks of Mannawar Tawi.

(vii) 127 Division Locating Battery had deployed a Sound Ranging Base in area Pt 994 extending north to south. A radar section for mortar locating was also deployed at Pt 994.

(F) Fire Direction Centre (FDC) Artillery

Located in Chhamb, closer to 5 Sikh HQ at Sakrana Ridge. The gun areas of 81 Field, 18 Field and 12 Field were in the rear of FDC. The HQ location of 191 Infantry Brigade was less than a km from FDC. Brigadier K Srinivasan with IO Captain Passi, Brigade Major (BM) Major AN Surya Narayan with G3 Captain Bali and survey troop commander Captain AK Kher were present in FDC. The Counter-bombardment command-post was alongside FDC which was manned by Captain Anil Khanna and Captain Akhilesh. The sparrow was Lt PK Sharma, EME Artillery Major Sekho and Education Officer Lt Daulat Ram were also present in the FDC complex. BHM Bhanwar Singh and 33 other ranks were part of the survey troop under the command of Captain Kher.

(G) Deployment of Armour

1. HQ of Armour Regiment 9 Deccan Horse was with 191 Infantry Brigade at Chhamb. The regiment had 2 squadrons west of Mannawar Tawi and 1 squadron at east of Mannawar Tawi.
2. 72 Armour Regiment was east of Mannawar Tawi on the home bank

(H) 10 Infantry Division Signal Unit was deployed in Akhnoor. They had established a signal centre and an exchange there, on which local and trunk lines were terminated. Speech circuits on line were available to HQ 15 Corps Udhampur, 28 and 191 Infantry Brigade HQs, 10 Artillery Brigade HQ and 61 Engineer Regiment.

In addition, a teleprinter circuit was available to HQ 15 Corps at Udhampur and telegraph circuits to the two infantry brigades. Hotlines were also provided to both infantry brigades and the artillery brigade HQs. Lines were also laid to 26 and 25 Infantry Divisions.

(I) 10 Infantry Division HQ was located at Akhnoor and a TAC HQ was set up near area Pallanwala. On 3rd December late in the afternoon, the GOC visited 191 Infantry Brigade HQ in Chhamb for a briefing. Late in the evening, GOC Major General Jaswant Singh with Lt Col Sabharwal CO 9 Para SF moved into TAC HQ as the battle commenced. However, ineffective communications and limited staff at the TAC HQ rendered it dysfunctional and the GOC was unable to deal with the battle for the next critical 24 hours.

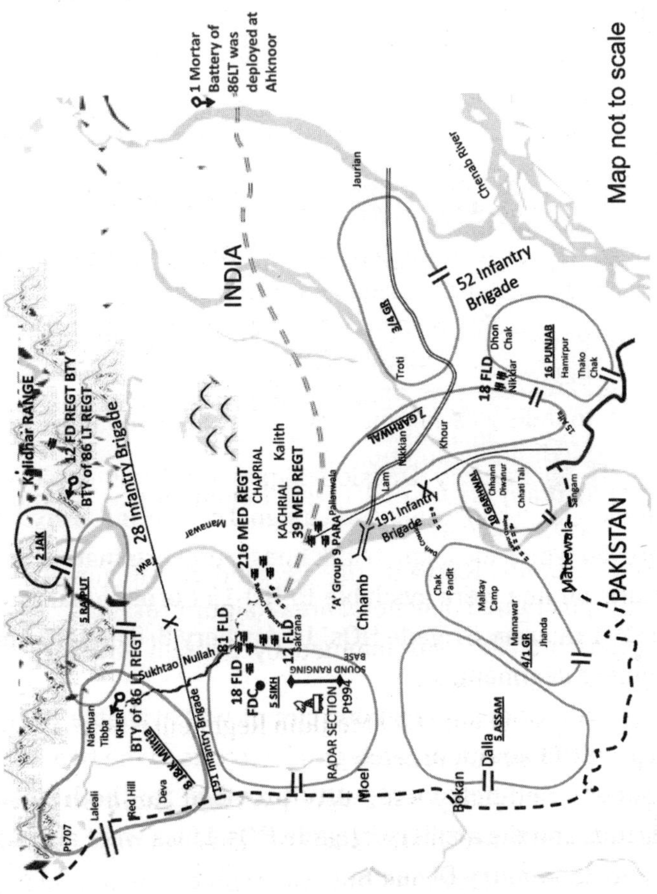

10 Artillery Brigade Deployment

Forward Observation Posts

Observation was provided for engagement of artillery fire and gaining enemy information as follows:

(i) Captain Sahi of 86 Light Regiment was positioned at Pt 707. He could engage targets from Kheri Battery.

(ii) Red Hill, Laleali was manned by Captain RI Singh of 39 Medium Regiment. Red Hill provided clear observation in depth and had the best view of the entire enemy area. Captain RI Singh was the authorised observation post officer of the Brigade and could direct the entire Brigade shooting without reference.

(iii) Captain Roshan Lal of 81 Field Regiment was positioned at Bokan.

(iv) Pir Jamal was manned by Captain Tyagi of 18 Field Regiment.

(v) Moel was manned by Captain R Kaura of 39 Medium Regiment.

(vi) Burejal was manned by Captain Jamwal of 81 Field Regiment.

(vii) Jhanda was manned by Lieutenant SN Singh of 39 Medium Regiment.

(viii) Captain Bhatia of 18 Field Regiment was positioned at Mannawar.

(ix) Captain Balwant of 39 Medium Regiment was positioned in general area Raipur Crossing.

(x) Chatti Tali was manned by Captain Sandhu of 81 Field Regiment.

(xi) Captain Paul of 39 Medium Regiment was positioned at Thako Chak area.

All OPs had bulky RS62 WWII version Radio Sets which used a 12 volt secondary battery. This set had a longer range for communications but was temperamental and less reliable. OPs also had AN/PRC 25 (Army Navy, Portable Radio, Communication) man-pack Radio Sets which were portable VHF FM combat net radio transreceivers. The solid state design of the AN/PRCs brought the weight down to less than 10 kg which included the battery. Its range was approximately 8 to 12km with standard antennas.

At FDC a consignment of AN/PRC batterys was received from 10 Div. HQ. This item being part of controlled stores, the Brigade Major did not issue these batteries to units fearing misuse. Due to this, at crucial stages of war, OPs did not have replacements for AN/PRC batteries, hampering operations.

In early November 1971, Captain AK Kher, the survey troop commander, had finished the survey of gun areas linking up with 25 and 26 Infantry Division. He had even set up observation stations at each BOP, covering all high ground areas from Laleali to Mannawar.

With the war clouds moving in, humour always found its way in through the form of unforgettable Munnu Swamy.

Mess staff Munnu Swamy of 127 Division Locating Battery showcased the humanity of Indian troops. Munnu Swamy normally worked as mess waiter and also officiated as Mess Havaldar. Munnu and cook John made a great team.

At Jaurian just before the war, Captain Kher asked Munnu Swamy, "If in war, you catch an enemy mess waiter as prisoner, what will you do to him?"

After a thought, he replied, "Sir, the poor man looks after his officers just like I do for you. I will give him some food and let him go quietly."

One day, Munnu Swamy was searching for something on the ground with a torchlight and at least 20 other men were helping him. Suddenly he quietly walked away and laughed,

"*Saala pata nahi kya dhund raha tha.*" That was Munnu Swamy from Kolar Goldfields of Karnataka.

It is pertinent to mention here that 127 Div. Loc had an important role in the 1965 war too. It operated the 3MK7F Mortar-locating radar which was of British origin. India was dependent on the British for its critical spares, but Britain had put a ban on military exports to India.

127 Div. Loc also had a recorder No. 5 for sound ranging, which was connected to microphones placed in a linear position on surveyed points. This would pick up the enemy gunfire sound and transmit it to the recorder, which would then print the sound pulses on a film.

Reading the time differences in sound meters would give the location of enemy guns. The most critical component of this recording system was a device called the grid, an electric-sensitive paper-thin device equal to the size of a rupee coin, which was supplied by Britain. Unfortunately there was no local manufacturing of this device.

Due to the ban, this critical component was not available, rendering most of the locating units out of service.

Fortunately in 1965, one Assistant Instructor Gunnery (AIG) of 127 Div. Loc had six of them hidden as reserves in his box. These grids made the 127 Division locating unit functional in war and an effective Indian counter bombardment could take place in defence of the Amritsar sector.

□

5

Pakistan's Offensive Plan

Pakistan's 23 Infantry Division under Major General Iftikar Khan Januja was tasked to advance to Akhnoor and capture Akhnoor Bridge. The Division had intense preparation and intelligence for offensive action and was deployed in its operational area of Bhimber.

Composition of 23 Infantry Division

(A) Infantry: Pakistan had 4 Infantry Brigades and one of them was an AK Brigade which was not well trained. Some additional infantry support from 17 Infantry Division was also available.

(i) 20 Infantry Brigade commanded by Brigadier Syed Hussain.

(ii) 66 Infantry Brigade commanded by Brigadier Qamar Khan.

(iii) 111 Infantry Brigade commanded by Brigadier Neseerulla Khan.

(iv) 4 AK Brigade commanded by Brigadier Ahmad Khan.

(B) Armour: 1 Regiment of 26 Cavalry of Sherman II Tanks integral to 23 Infantry Div. 1 Armoured Brigade comprising of 2 Regiments of T59 tanks, 11 and 28 Cavalry commanded by Brigadier Sardar Ahmed.

(C) Artillery: Division Artillery and some additional Corps Artillery commanded by Brigadier Naseer Khan.

4 Field Regiments, 1 Composite Regiment, 2 Medium Regiments, 2 sections of heavy guns (155); in all, about 195 guns with one Division-locating battery.

(D) A Section of Air observation post based on fixed wing aircraft

(E) Air Support: Three squadrons of F-86E/F Saber at Sargodha, Murid and Peshawar made up the fighter element for air support to 23 Infantry Division.

Pakistan's attack plan was for 4 AK Brigade with Armour Regiment to advance through the north via the Sukhtau Nullah and to establish a bridge head on Mandiala Crossing and capture Kachrial Chaprial heights.

111 Infantry Brigade group was tasked to attack the Indian posts from Pir Jamal to Moel area.

66 Infantry Brigade with Armour was to break through from Burejal to Moel area and capture Chhamb.

20 Infantry Brigade with armour support was directed to attack from Jhanda to Mannawar in the south and capture Raipur and Darh Crossing.

□

6

Prior to War
The Situation on Indian Side

There were many indications of Pakistani build up along the BOPs. It was noticed that Pakistani patrols included some members in Black Dungarees and Black Berets which indicated presence of Armoured Corps reconnaissance parties. This was duly reported by Artillery OPs.

Infantry, which was deployed in section strengths along with the BSF on each BOP, did not report these developments. Even if some did report, their channel was too cumbersome for the flow of information to reach 10 Infantry Division HQ.

All Artillery forward observation-post officers deployed on BOPs reported Pakistani patrolling and reconnaissance in their areas to HQ 10 Artillery Brigade and the input was further transmitted to 10 Infantry Division HQ.

There was a hue and cry at HQ 10 Infantry Division about the scare mongering by the Artillery when the Infantry was not reporting such movements.

Only after the 9 Para SF deep-penetration patrol reported Pakistani armour buildup and preparation for the attack, the two Brigadiers from 191 Infantry Brigade were assigned to visit a few BOPs on the CFL and report their assessment to 10 Div. HQ.

On 1st/2nd December, Brigadier Satish Mathur and Brigadier Jasbir Singh visited the BOPs. On such a visit to Jhanda post, Lieutenant SN Singh the OP officer from 39 Medium himself pointed out the direction and location of 8 enemy tanks opposite Jhanda area. The Brigadiers now observed for themselves the enemy's armoured deployment. However the Brigadiers assessed that the enemy was just showboating but did assure anti-tank support to the infantry units.

At the same time, Captain AK Kher was establishing control points in enemy territory in order to provide theatre grid survey to guns in case of forward deployment of the Artillary Brigade. The two Brigadiers, without knowing the purpose of Captain AK Kher's task, reported to the GOC that 10 Artillery Brigade's survey troop commander was exposing 10 Div. plans to the enemy.

On 2nd December, 1971, Captain AK Kher was called in the evening to meet his Brigade commander, Brigadier Henry Srinivasan, who was in the 39 Medium Regiment location. While proceeding towards the location, Captain Kher met Captain Kamal Bakshi with Subedar Assa Singh of 5 Sikh in Gopar area, where they were laying minefields.

Upon reaching 39 Medium location, Captain AK Kher met the unit Adjutant Captain Pande who informed him that Brigadier Srinivasan was furious and all knives were out. The Brigadier was sitting with CO 39 Medium Lt Col Gauri Shankar in the command post vehicle and upon Captain AK Kher's entry, shouted, "What the hell have you been doing, you bloody rascal!" Captain AK Kher then took out the survey map and spread it in front of him and informed him, "I have fixed all OP locations on a theatre grid and have carried forward theatre grid by fixing control points in enemy territory to facilitate our future deployment of guns while advancing."

The Commander asked for further explanation and Captain AK Kher complied. Brigadier Srinivasan retorted, "Who the hell ordered this to be done?" Captain AK Kher replied, "My professional ethics dictated such a move!"

The temper of the Brigadier abated and he ordered a drink and personally served Captain Kher and told the CO 39, "Gauri, I have been telling you that this chap is too good. The GOC did not understand what this chap was doing." Captain Kher was invited to join the Commander for dinner later.

Intelligence Summary (ISUM)

There was an ISUM circulated from HQ 10 Infantry DIV, marked Class B info.

"Pakistan Armoured Brigade strength observed in Khariwal."

GOC Major General Jaswant Singh personally noted in green ink on the ISUM:

"Exaggerated info; don't expect more than a squadron."

The Pakistanis' deployment of their guns, dumping of ammunition and concentration of Infantry was totally concealed from Indian eyes.

From the Indian side, we did not employ TAC R(Tactical Reconnaissance) or ARTY R(Artillery Reconnaissance) via the IAF to gain information.

HQ 10 Infantry Division refused to read the battle indications prior to war and the buzzword in Div. HQ was, 'We will clobber them!'

□

7

Outbreak of Hostilities

In the evening at 1700 hrs, on 3rd December, 1971 the scene at Fire Direction Center was as follows. The Brigade Major, Major Surya Narayan ordered the staff to pack up the FDC and move to Troti Heights as there was a change in plans.

The FDC location at Troti had been examined earlier during the day by Captain Khanna and Captain Kher. All FDC staff started packing up in order to prepare for the move.

Unknown to FDC, at 1740 hrs, Pakistan carried out air strikes on Indian airfields and radar installations at Amritsar, Faridkot, Halwara, Sirsa, Pathankot, Srinagar, Agra, Jamnagar and Jodhpur.

At about 1900 hrs, the attack news filtered in and the Brigade Major announced, "Gentlemen, the war has broken out; stay put at the current FDC."

The FDC now had to be redug and communications re-established by sparrow Lt PK Sharma and his assistant, Subedar Khrup. Immediately, all Artillery units were issued a warning order.

Meanwhile, Pakistani radio news bulletins announced air attacks by the Indian Air Force on their airfields. This news was heard by Captain Kher on a Sony Transistor, which was the only transistor radio in FDC.

Reports from forward observation posts were tense and reported total lack of Pakistani movement.

28 Infantry Brigade Sector was hilly and had protective minefields. Specifically 8 J & K Militia had well-developed wire obstacle systems in front of their localities and the main approaches of Pt 707, Laleali, Red Hill and Dewa were well protected.

191 Infantry Brigade Sector was favourable for armoured battle, more so for Pakistan, due to favourable terrain on their side.

5 Sikh were well dug in with protective minefields and had cat-wire entanglements in front of their battalion area.

5 Assam from Jhanda to Barsala were dug in, but there were no protective minefields or any wire obstacles; the gap was deliberately left at two specific places in 5 Assam area to enable 68 Infantry Brigade to advance into Pakistan in an attack plan.

4/1 Gorkha were well dug in and had protective minefields and cat-wire obstacles.

10 Garhwal were also well dug in and had protective minefields and cat-wire obstacles.

Armoured Regiment

There were 3 squadrons of 9 Deccan Horse, one in Gogi-Barsala area to support 5 Assam, one at Chhamb area to support 5 Sikh and one squadron east of Mannawar Tawi in depth of which a troop of 3 tanks was deployed near Chhamb bridge for its protection.

The commanding officer of Deccan Horse Lt Col Bal was an aggressive tank commander but unfortunately had met with an accident a few days earlier and was out of action. Now the Regiment was commanded by the 2IC Major HN Hoon.

Captain Kaushik was Adjutant of the Regiment and Captain Divender Singh, who was a company mate of Captain Kher at OTS, was a part of the unit.

Units in 52 Infantry Brigade Sector were well dug in with protective cat-wire in front and marshy land, making the location a natural barrier, unfavourable for enemy armoured attack.

□

8

Pakistan's Offensive at Chhamb

While India was preparing for the attack **on 3rd December, 1971, at 2042 hrs,** the enemy launched a pre-emptive attack starting with heavy concentration of artillery fire which was directed simultaneously on all Indian BOPs, Forward Defended Locations(FDLs) and defences. There was heavy enemy bombardment for 5 or 6 hours, and there after all BOPs were under full-fledged assault by about 20,000 Pakistani infantry alongwith armoured support.

The BSF post immediately withdrew, creating a gap between Pir Jamal and Red Hill.

Situation at 28 Infantry Brigade Sector:

Pt 707, Laleali, Red Hill and Dewa immediately came under attack. The strength of the enemy attack was such that a platoon of 8 J & K Militia at Red Hill was evacuated as it was an isolated feature and not in mutual support of Laleali. The infantry troops of Major Virendra of 8 J & K Militia fell back to Laleali.

Artillery OP Captain RI Singh of 39 Medium who was at Red Hill also pulled back to Laleali which was north of Red Hill and directed defensive fire from there. Believe it or not, in the 1965 operations, a newly commissioned Second Lieutenant RI Singh, silver gunner from School of Artillery was OP officer at

Red Hill, wounded while fighting and a captured Prisoner of War.

This time CO Lt Col Gauri Shankar's orders were clear: 'RI, don't get captured!'

Down at Dewa Hill feature, 8 J & K Militia company of Captain Mandal was isolated and a major focus of Pakistani assault, but the initial enemy attack was beaten back successfully by Captain Mandal.

There were repeated assaults on Pt 707 by the enemy's 2AK Battalion and Zhob Militia supported by intense Pakistani artillery and mortar fire. These were repulsed throughout the 4th of December by Major Sharma and his troops, but the enemy regrouped with additional force every time.

The enemy in bigger numbers replacing the Zhob Militia with a properly trained battalion, was able to break through. There were pitched battles for hours before the enemy wrested a foothold in the forward trenches of 8 J & K Militia at Pt 707.

Captain Sahi of 86 Light Regiment was the Artillary OP officer at Pt 707 and he was supported by Kheri Battery of 86 Light with the rest of the Artillery brigade in range. Captain Sahi fired around 1,300 rounds from his Kheri Battery to protect Pt 707 but when Peepa LP ammunition ran out, he was handicapped.

The enemy was now close to delivering the final assault. Sahi had to call for Medium support as a last resort and took shots from 39 Medium guns. The accurate fire from 39 Medium decimated the enemy and saved the day.

Major Sharma's Infantry troops of 8 J & K Militia held ground and successfully repulsed all assaults.

Lt Col Jasbir Pal Singh Randhawa, commanding officer 8 J & K Militia, was incidentally visiting Pt 707 with his Ghatak (commando) platoon and stayed on at Pt 707 till the end of operations. He later earned a VrC for it.

The enemy now shifted focus from Pt 707 and carried out reinforced and repeated assaults on picket Laleali. The enemy, after a repeated number of assaults finally managed to cross cat-wire obstacles and protective minefields and almost reached the top of Laleali picket shouting, "*Hindustani kutton, bhag jao*."

Captain RI Singh of 39 Medium, who was the OP officer this time, was not going to be captured, like in 1965.

In the 1965 war, Second Lieutenant RI Singh lay wounded with grievous injuries and it was difficult for his Radio Operator, Gurcharan Singh, to evacuate him in the condition he was in. The option of carrying the officer down to safety would expose the whole team and delay evacuation. Second Lieutenant RI Singh ordered his OP party to leave him behind as he would be a liability and instead try to get back by stealth and get assistance. This was the bravest thing RI could do under the circumstances. Unfortunately before Gurcharan Singh could come back, the enemy had picked up Second Lieutenant RI Singh and taken him POW.

Now in 1971, Captain RI Singh, for the love of God and Country, returned to the same area after six years and volunteered to be OP at the same point, displaying tremendous courage and guts. However, he found himself in a similar situation; only this time history was not going to be repeated with RI He responded with "*Bole So Nihaal, Sat Sri Akal*" and asked for red over red, which meant bombard my position – a defence of the last resort.

Red over red is not allowed with mediums as it amounts to suicide. All defence works and bunkers get destroyed and one's own forces face a huge risk of suffering casualties. Captain RI Singh, however, did not have an alternative.

On Captain RI's orders, 39 Medium Regiment Guns opened up on his own position to stop the enemy from overrunning it.

And thereafter, there was only stunning silence. All radio communications at FDC went quiet for a few minutes.

The radio cracked up with Captain RI Singh shouting, "Attack destroyed, stand easy!" Medium fire on RI's own location destroyed the Pakistani assault totally with 50 or more enemy lying dead, including the Pakistani company commander who led the attack. Thus aided by the heroism of Captain RI Singh and the firepower of 39 Medium, Major Virendra's company of 8 J & K Militia survived, held on to Laleali post and lost no ground. Major Virendra Singh Sahi went on to earn a VrC.

In the meantime, an enemy Air OP was also hit by AD fire but he managed to cross back to Pakistani territory.

After no success at Laleali and Pt 707, the enemy, suffering heavy casualties, regrouped and increased the volume of troops to 2 full Battalions, attacking Dewa with heavy mortar and Artillery support repeateadly. Finally, the tenacity of the enemy paid off. A depleted Captain Mandal, with his company, fell back to Dewa waterpoint after inflicting heavy casualties on the enemy and occupied defences there. Dewa Hill was captured by the enemy.

Captain Mandal's company held their ground at Dewa waterpoint defences till the end of operations, repulsing a number of Pakistani assaults.

An enemy platoon of 6 AK Battalion succeeded in infiltrating location Kheri, where a Battery of 86 Lt Regiment was deployed and managed to attack the wagon lines. A company of 5 Rajput, which was deployed at Nathuan Tibba, counter attacked and evicted the enemy, causing heavy casualties.

28 Brigade defences in Laleali, Pt 707, Dewa waterpoint and Nathuan Tibba lay intact and the troops bravely stood their ground under heavy enemy assault.

There was minimum action on Kalidhar-Katau area as it was mountainous.

Situation at 191 Infantry Brigade sector

10 Garhwal Regiment Locations

No physical assault was delivered on 10 Garhwal locations,

but the enemy brought down heavy Artillery fire on 15 Alfa and Garadh posts. They formed up a few times at Nadala and Marchola, but were repelled by accurate Artillery fire. 15 Alfa post was vacated.

4/1 Gorkha Regiment Locations

Bhusa: The Post was withdrawn and immediately overrun by the enemy armour and infantry. Second Lieutenant AGJ Swittens who along with his buddy Narjang Gurung were dug in a foxhole close to the CFL to observe the enemy. His AN/PRC Radio ran out of battery and he could not be informed by this Company Commander to withdraw. By the time he realised what was going on the enemy had already overrun his position, he got captured and taken in as POW. His buddy trying to save his officer attacked the enemy with his Khukri and was killed in action.

Jhanda: Major Rajinder's company was deployed at Jhanda, which was a high ground with a few houses and a big mango tree. It was 900 to 1200 yards from CFL and was under heavy enemy bombardment, but no physical assault was delivered. A couple of times enemy tanks formed up for assault and these assaults were effectively thwarted by accurate Artillery fire by OP Lieutenant SN Singh of 39 Medium. He dominated the area by observation and fire. His code name was 55 for radio communications.

Lieutenant SN Singh had established his observation post on top of the mango tree. Kabul Singh, his radio operator, had made a rope ladder for him and a seat on the top, well camouflaged! He maintained his Radio and line from a trench dug in the ground.

There was a heavy demand for Medium gun fire from all Brigade OPs to stop the onslaught of enemy tanks. Usually an

OP had to direct a battery of guns but due to serious demands from all round, the CFL, SN Singh only had a 3 gun troop dedicated to him. SN made up the deficit by firing so rapidly that this equalled the shelling capacity of 6.

A squadron of enemy tanks with Infantry was operating against Jhanda. On each formation of assault, Lieutenant SN would radio "55 for 43" (43 being the gun position), "TGT M 5523, enemy tanks and infantry forming up, six rounds gunfire." In response, 36 rounds of Medium fire, emulating a 6 Gun Battery, would land on the enemy. The enemy would take casualties and abandon the attack. He repulsed 10 to 15 such attacks while his own post was under constant shelling. He took a stand for his men and post and did not budge from the treetop.

Most unassuming and soft-spoken, Lieutenant SN Singh was a great footballer, famous in the unit for centre-line reverse kick goal. His game at volleyball was also noteworthy with his impeccable placing and volley. SN was called Shambhu the Great, by Captain Kher, his close buddy. SN has four wonderful children who are all dedicated to Defence Services.

Aided by Lieutenant SN Singh, Major Rajinder's company of 4/1 Gorkha held on to the post.

Mangotia: A section of Major Rajinder's company under Second Lieutenant Prakash Chand Singh Khati was at Mangotia post, which came under heavy repeated enemy assaults on the 3rd, 5th and 6th of December. These assaults were supported by armour and accurate Artillery fire. Each time the enemy was beaten back with Second Lieutenant Khati holding on. Khati was awarded the VrC for displaying courage and leadership.

Mannawar: On Mannawar, no physical assault was delivered. The enemy formed up a couple of times but was dispersed by our accurate Artillery fire directed by Captain

Bhatia of 18 Field. The enemy was relentless with Mortar and HMG firing. Major DP Lakhanpal, the company commander, went to personally man an MMG even though he should not have. The enemy HMG blast directly hit his bunker and got him through the loop, killing him instantly.

Artillery OP Captain Bhatia of 18 Field, who was in location, continuously took accurate shots and thwarted the enemy from advancing. The position was secure and retained.

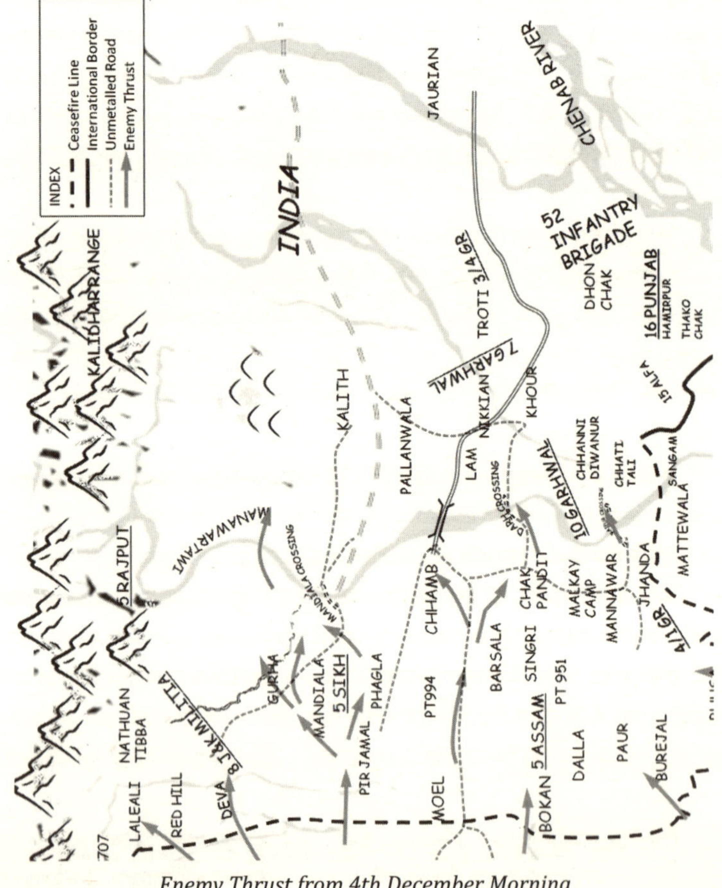

Enemy Thrust from 4th December Morning

Bullet-ridden Mannawar School

Malkay Camp: A company was deployed in Malkay Camp area and came under some enemy Artillery fire but it was also well dug in and secure as it was a depth location.

Chak Pandit: A company under Major Gian Singh, along with Battalion HQ, was deployed in Chak Pandit area and came under some enemy Artillery fire but was well dug in and secure, as it was a depth location.

Mattewala Action in 4/1 GR Location

Mattewala Tower was an elevated man-made structure setup by the Pakistanis on the Mattewala Ridge and it provided information to observers about our depth areas.

On 4th December morning, CO 39 Lt Col Gauri Shankar took one 5.5 Inch Medium gun to Mannawar by crossing over the Chhamb bridge. Heading the gun detachment was Hav Piara Singh of 393 Medium Battery and the driver of the Kraz was Lanc Naik (L/Nk) Gurcharan Singh (Buda) of 123 Medium Battery. They managed to securely take the gun under heavy enemy observed fire and deployed in Mannawar area. About 20 rounds of 80-pounders were fired on Mattewala in direct shooting using HE 117 fuse.

Mattewala Observation Tower was damaged and it tilted heavily. Six enemy bunkers were also destroyed. Hav Piara Singh was mentioned in dispatches. Lt Col Gauri Shankar was a courageous and exemplary commanding officer and was decorated with the VSM immediately after the war.

5.5 Inch Gun of 39 Medium Regiment

5 Sikh Regiment Locations

Pir Jamal was manned by a platoon of 5 Sikh with Artillery OP Captain Tyagi of 18 Field. They withdrew on 3rd night, as this post was away from the main area. Brigade Major Major Surya Narayan ordered Captain AK Kher to pickup Captain Tyagi from Gopar area while heavy enemy shelling was going on. Captain Kher brought him to his Battery deployed in Sakrana.

Mandiala North came under heavy bombardment. Mandiala was very thinly held and Major Ram Chandran did not have anti-tank measures to engage the armoured thrust. Neither did he have any Medium Machine Gun (MMG) to engage the enemy infantry nor was he given any Artillery OP support to halt the advancing enemy. The enemy facing least resistance bypassed Mandiala on 4th December. The higher ups had not foreseen that the enemy would penetrate via Peer Jamal Dewa belt and use the Sukhtau Nullah to advance.

Captain Kamal Bakshi and Subedar Assa Singh were still laying minefields, and were captured by the enemy as they were caught by surprise upon the unexpectedly swift arrival of the enemy and were taken in as POWs.

Brigadier Mathur, an Armoured Corps officer, who was taking over 191 Infantry Brigade, in sand model discussions had vehemently ruled out the tankability of Sukhtau Nullah. Major Ranbir of 39 Medium Regiment, who had fought the 1965 war in Chhamb, repeatedly told him that the enemy armour came in via Sukhtau Nullah in 1965. This prudent advice was completely disregarded by Brigadier Mathur and Mandiala North was kept thinly defended.

Moel

Captain Ravinder Kaura of 39 Medium was the Artillery OP officer at Moel with 5 Sikh. On 4th December, the Moel post was repeatedly assaulted by 4 Punjab and 6 AK Battalions of Pakistan with covering fire from their Cavalry. Relentless attacks by the enemy were repulsed by effective artillery fire brought down by Captain Kaura, inflicting 25 enemy casualties. 5 Sikh held on to the post.

Finally, the persistent Pakistanis bypassed Moel via the gap created due to withdrawal of Pir Jamal and shortly thereafter established contact with Pt 994 (303 on metre grid) and engaged the company of Major DS Pannu. Realising this, Captain Kaura and his section tried to withdraw to Pt 994 to avoid being cut from the back by the enemy. En route, he was ambushed along with his OP party and their hands were bound. On orders of the Pakistani officer, the entire section was machine gunned. His radio operator, Bhajan Singh, was hit on the arm and was left as dead by the Pakistanis but he regained consciousness and managed to reach 39 Medium gun area, severely wounded. He reported that Captain Kaura was grievously wounded and asking for water but could not be helped and hence he was presumed to be killed. Captain Kaura was awarded the VrC posthumously. It was subsequently learned that wounded Captain Kaura was held POW and kept in some prison in Pakistan.

Pt 994: OP officer Captain AS Malik of 39 Medium was under orders from CO 39 to relieve Captain R Kaura positioned at Moel. When he reached Pt 994 from 39 Medium Gun area in Kachrial, Moel was already under enemy attack. Major Pannu advised Captain AS Malik not to proceed to Moel but Captain Malik disregarded his advice and proceeded to Moel with his OP party. Thereafter nothing was ever heard of Captain AS Malik and his OP party.

Moel was Major Pannu's BOP. The company deployed at Pt 994 was commanded by Major DS Pannu, who was an instructor in OTS when Captain AK Kher was in training in 1968. The Pakistanis, after overrunning Moel, arrived at Pt 994 in full strength. The enemy formed up repeatedly at Pt 994 forward location with their Artillery support and among the battle cries of "Allah O Akbar", but were engaged by Pannu effectively. Physically no Pakistani assault was delivered on Pt 994.

Repeated attacks were formed by the Pakistanis to dislodge Major Pannu, who was unmindful of his own safety and kept moving from one position to another, holding the post until 5th December. Finally a direct hit of Pakistani Artillery on Major Pannu's bunker killed him, leaving the company leaderless.

Captain AS Malik of 39 Medium who had proceeded from location of Pt 994 towards Moel. He was also presumed killed. The enemy was able to temporarily take Pt 994.

An immediate counter attack was conducted by Adjutant of 9 Deccan Horse, Captain Surendra Kaushik on Pt 994, with a platoon of 5 Sikh. He was supported by Artillery OP Captain Mathur of 81 Field who brought down accurate Artillery fire and restored the situation at Pt 994 (.303 on metre grid), causing heavy losses to the enemy with 9 tanks and 3 RCLs destroyed. Captain Kaushik was awarded the VrC for his actions. Major DS Pannu was also awarded the VrC posthumously for bravery.

The Radar section of 127 Div. Loc Battery deployed at Pt 994 became vulnerable and was not tenable in the current location in this situation.

Phagla Ridge

At Phagla, the company was commanded by Major Jaivir Singh. The enemy launched repeated attacks supported by Armour and Artillery fire. The enemy managed to break through and a fierce hand-to-hand battle ensued on this post. Jaivir held his ground, inflicting heavy losses on the enemy. When the enemy penetrated into company defences, Sepoy Rachpal shot and bayoneted three Pakistani soldiers. Major Jaivir was awarded the MvC and Rachpal the VrC. Captain Sukhwant Singh Gill, who was commanding a Battery of 18 Field, moved towards Phagla to employ accurate artillery fire to stabilise the situation there. He was also awarded the VrC.

MMG of Alfa Group deployed near Chhamb Bridge

Even 5 Sikh CO Lt Col PK Khanna was decorated with MvC for exemplary skill and courage in defending the area.

Sakrana came under heavy bombardment but no physical assault was delivered and was bypassed by the enemy.

On the night of 4th December, 1971, a small scouting force of Pakistani infantry of 13 AK and 47 Punjab Battalion of 4 AK Brigade with 6 to 7 tanks managed to advance towards Sukhtau Nullah due to the gap created between Pir Jamal and Red Hill on the CFL. They then proceeded unimpeded via Gopar towards Mandiala Crossing. This was a textbook repeat of the 1965 Pakistani operation.

The enemy's infantry advance party, which was moving ahead of the tanks, managed to infiltrate Chhamb Bridge. Alpha group of 9 Para SF, which was deployed at the junction of Sukhtau Nullah and Mannawar Tawi close to the bridge for its defence, made contact with initial elements of Pakistani Infantry halting them on the bridge itself.

Six to seven tanks of the initial Pakistani probe also now advanced via Sukhtau Nullah and reached the Crossing. They were promptly identified and destroyed by Medium Artillery fire in a direct shooting role and by ATGMs of 12 Guards. These were Captain Puri's boys, who were positioned at the Banks of Mannawar Tawi at the Crossing.

L/Nk Nar Bahadur Chhetri of 12 Guards single-handedly destroyed two enemy tanks by advancing 200 metres ahead of his position, fully exposed, accurately engaging the two tanks and knocking them out. L/Nk Nar Bahadur Chhetri was decorated with the MvC for his actions.

The rest of the enemy tanks were knocked out by Medium Artillary fire.

Depth company of 4/1 Gorkha deployed at Chak Pandit was led by Major Gian Singh. He, being closest to Mandiala from the south side, was now ordered to counter attack Mandiala North and plug the gap in 5 Sikh location. Unfortunately, as Major Gian Singh and his platoon were setting out, they came under accurate heavy Pakistani shelling, injuring Major Gian Singh and killing his JCO N/Sub HB Thapa. This stalled the counter attack and subsequently no counter attack could take place to evict the enemy. The enemy now had a reasonable foothold in Mandiala North area.

Situation in Artillery FDC

On the night of 3rd December some enemy shells landed on FDC. Fortunately they got 'tree-burst' as FDC was situated in a thick mango grove. The majority of enemy shells were landing short of FDC on 5 Sikh locations or going over and landing on other targets. Brigadier Srinivasan was present in FDC and issuing instructions to staff and various units. Brigade Major Major Surya Narayan was controlling fire and maintaining the shooting map. Captain Bali was manning D-5 (Brigade Firing Net) and Captain Kher was manning fire order line to all units. All throughout the 3rd December night all the staff were busy controlling and organising defensive fire tasks for the entire 10 Infantry Division frontages.

The situation at FDC was very tense and cigarettes were in short supply. Captain Kher was used to only smoking Gold Flake King Size cigarettes. Brigadier Henry asked for a fag, which was promptly offered to him and thereafter the commander instructed Captain Kher to leave the packet on the table. The pack of smokes was finished by dawn. It was the only pack of cigarettes he had. Alas, Captain Kher was left without a smoke for remainder of the war!

Captain Kher's survey troops had dug in on Sakrana Ridge just ahead of 81 Field Regiment gun area. At 0600 hrs on 4th December, after the previous night of bombardment, Captain AK Kher went to check each trench and his men. He ordered all personal weapons to be cleaned with magazines unloaded, ammunition cleaned and reloaded. Each man was carrying four loaded magazines and two HE36 hand grenades.

After checking all his men and making sure all was okay, Captain Kher asked his orderly Dev Raj for the shaving kit. Dev Raj was extremely surprised and said, "*Sahib, ladai mein* shave?" As Captain Kher was soaping his face, a enemy salvo landed short of his position. Captain Kher was shaving his right cheek when another salvo went over and landed in gun area of 81 Field. All of a sudden, a heavy roar of enemy gunfire was heard and Captain Kher immediately jumped into the trench, with a rain of shells starting to land on the survey troop and 81 Field locations.

Captain Kher successfully managed to complete his shave in the trench which was now covered with mud and dust. This firing lasted for three to four hours with intermittent pauses. By the time firing stopped, Captain Kher's trench had completely caved in. His ears, eyes, nostrils were full of muck and his helmet had splinter dents. Fortunately Captain Kher's survey troops did not have any casualties. In this enemy firing, one gun of 81 Field Regiment was badly damaged and also a few casualties were reported.

At approximately 0915 hours on 4th December, two IAF SU-7 aircraft flew over Chhamb to attack enemy positions in a ground support role to the joy of our men on the ground, but regrettably one SU-7 was immediatly shot down by the enemy AA fire, making the situation even more tense.

Later in the morning, Brigade Major Major Surya Narayan assigned Captain Kher to check the state of ALG at Rakhmuti. To reach Rakhmuti from FDC, Captain Kher had to cross Chhamb Bridge area, which was under severe enemy shelling. Just a little earlier it had received a few direct hits, one 1-ton vehicle of 12 Field was destroyed with two men lying dead on the bridge along with an unexploded medium shell. Despite the odds, Captain Kher managed to reach Rakhmuti safely. He found the ALG to be safe and reported no damage back to FDC. He proceeded to 89 Field workshop where he met OC Major Iyer, Captain Kalia, Captain Grover and Lieutenant Bala. The officers at the workshop treated Captain Kher and his escort party of seven to eight men, including the driver Atequidil Narayan Tanghapan Nair (ANT in short) to tea and biscuits. After completing the mission, Captain Kher led his men back to FDC.

On the morning of 5th December, Captain Kher was assigned by Brigade Major to go to 12 Field regiment gun area with the fire plan. Captain Kher, under heavy shelling reached 12 Field HQ and met 2IC Major Dua. He thereafter headed to the gun area where 12 Field was constantly engaging enemy targets and raining fire on the enemy. Captain Kher met Lieutenant Khajuria, the GPO, and handed over the fire plans for his execution. Khajuria was gracious enough to offer

Captain Kher some *puri* and *sabzi* along with tea as Captain Kher had not eaten a proper meal since 3rd December lunch.

Upon returning back to FDC Captain Kher heard the following enemy communication on the Rear Link Net between an enemy tank-troop leader with his Commanding Officer.

Papa 1: " *Samnay ridge line par dushman ka OP lagta hai.*"

CO: "Get back, lower the hull, observe carefully and engage."

CO: "These bloody Mediums are playing merry hell into us."

25 Pounder Field Gun in action

CO: "I want no casualties, bloody well be careful."

This communication was reported to Brigadier Srinavasan by Captain Kher.

At night, when every soul was staying put at one place securely inside a bunker, the Brigade Major again ordered Captain Kher to go back under enemy shelling to check the aircraft and its security at ALG at Rakhmuti, a distance of 20 km.

The initial enemy probe by now had infiltrated north Mandiala and the area was very strained. The road was littered with ammunition vehicles, either destroyed or abandoned, and small arms firing happening all around. Captain Kher and the escort party overcame the obstacles due to their intimate knowledge of the terrain and reached Rakhmuti. There was no aircraft at ALG, contrary to the Brigade Major's expectations. Captain Kher on his part made sure that necessary security was in place when the aircraft arrived. Having completed the task, he then drove back into hotbed Chhamb at night.

5 Assam Regiment Locations

The dummy minefield gap between Jhanda and Barsala was marked by a single strand of wire; this gap was protected by a squadron of 9 Deccan Horse positioned at Barsala and a section of ATGM's of 12 Guards.

There were 3 BOPs in front of 5 Assam. Paur was manned by BSF and a platoon of 5 Assam led by Captain KS Rathod. Burejal was manned by BSF along with a platoon commanded by Captain GR Singh with Captain DS Jamwal of 81 Field Regiment being the Artillery OP officer and Bokan, manned by a platoon of 5 Assam, led by Captain Kutt with Captain Roshan Lal of 81 Field as Artillery OP. A section was also posted at Dalla Post.

Upon the onset of hostilities, Bokan was heavily shelled. As the balloon went up, Artillery OP Captain Roshan withdrew along with the platoon of 5 Assam to main defences. Bokan was immediately overrun by the Pakistani 66 Infantry Brigade.

Dalla Post came under heavy Pakistani shelling and was pulverised. The platoon was depleted and withdrew.

BSF evacuated the Paur post immediately on 3rd December night. However Captain Rathod and his platoon continued to offer resistance. Ultimately though on 4th December morning, the enemy captured Paur with Captain KS Rathod presumed killed.

Enemy attention was now focused on Burejal. The post was manned by a platoon led by Captain GR Singh with Artillery

OP Captain Jamwal who were well entrenched. They gave stiff resistance to multiple assaults by the Pakistanis. Captain Jamwal broke up the initial assaults by bringing down accurate Artillery fire all day on the 4th and did not allow the enemy to deliver a physical attack. However the post took casualties and stood depleted. The enemy could no longer be held back and finally broke through with much higher numbers in spite of suffering significant casualties caused by Jamwal's fire. Finally the persistent enemy broke through and Captain Jamwal, out of desperation, had to call for defensive fire, red over red over red on his position to halt the advance. They held on for a short while but eventually on 5th December, Burejal fell.

Captain Jamwal's last radio call to his Battery was, "Tell Tiger to look after my family!"

Captain DS Jamwal, Captain GR Singh and 19 ORs were valiantly killed in hand-to-hand combat.

After ceasefire (CF), the Pakistani company commander, who had captured Burejal, was given one of the Jurrat medal by Pakistan. The officer confirmed that Captain Jamwal had shot two Pakistani NCOs and the Pakistani officer, in vengeance, shot Captain Jamwal dead. Major AK Suri, Quarter Master of 5 Assam, rushed in a convoy of 3 or 4 vehicles with reinforcements to Burejal but was ambushed by the enemy and presumed killed on the 5th December. Later it came to light that an injured Major Ashok Suri was taken POW.

After the collapse of BOPs, the enemy infantry advanced to main 5 Assam defended locations along with armour. The advance somewhat got halted on the barbed wire, marking the minefields.

The determined enemy, after probing, found out that the minefields were dummy and a full-fledged concentrated assault was launched on 5 Assam main locations. After repeated assaults, Gogi was captured. On 5th December, Major Makin, the company commander whose platoon had withdrawn to Barsala, counter attacked Gogi to regain the position, but was killed along with 8 ORs. Major Makin's tenacity angered the enemy so much that his mortal remains were mutilated by them. With the counter attack having failed, the enemy marched towards Barsala.

Major Mukhtiar Singh positioned at Singri was tasked by the CO Lt Col Malhi to launch a fresh counter attack to regain Major Makin's platoon area and was given a 3 Tank support from 72 Armoured regiment which was freshly introduced into the battle by the Div. Commander on the 4th evening. Major Mukhtiar with 3 of his remaining Platoons counter attacked Barsala and temporarily regained the area causing heavy casualties on the enemy but they could only hold the enemy back for a day.

Now overwhelmed, 5 Assam did not make an effective use of their Recoil Less (RCL) guns to engage Pakistani tanks. 5 Assam suffered heavy casualties with 6 officers, Major

RCL Gun used in 1971

JBS Makin, Major Ashok Suri (QM), Captain Giri Raj Singh, Captain KS Rathod, Captain PN Kutt, Lieutenant O Wilson and approximately 50 other ranks killed, leaving the battalion leaderless and routed.

The CO Lt Col Malhi personally tried his best to redeploy his withdrawing battalion in Singri depth area, but his men did not stay and retreated back to main defences at Troti Heights.

This Pakistani action completely dispersed 5 Assam and created a wide gap between the defences of 5 Sikh and 4/1 Gorkha, who were effectively resisting repeated Pakistani attacks till then.

The advancing Pakistani column was checked by intervention of 9 Deccan Horse at Barsala, but there was no local counter attack mounted by 4/1 Gorkha or 5 Sikh to restore the situation in 5 Assam areas. The enemy was thus able to take Singri too.

Dispersing of 5 Assam totally and the enemy capturing Mandiala North in 5 Sikh location unhinged the defences of Chhamb and cut it open.

Now 4/1 Gorkha battalion HQ reported to 191 Brigade HQ of heavy casualties based on some misinformation and disruption in communication with its company. They started withdrawing from Chak Pandit and abandoned a well-entrenched location of Malkay Camp due to the danger of being outflanked by the enemy via Singri. Thus 4/1 Gorkha also withdrew to main defences at Troti/ Dhon Chak area. The casualties of 4/1 Gorkha were two Officer, one JCO and one Jawan.

Lieutenant SN Singh Artillery OP held on with Kabul Singh at Jhanda and called on Radio, "55 FOR 1(1 is CO), MY FRIENDS ARE LEAVING. WHAT ARE THE ORDERS FOR ME?"

"1(CO) FOR 55, RUN FASTER THAN THEM," was the CO's reply.

Uptill now 5 Sikh positions were mostly intact and defended tenaciously. However, they also started to withdraw to main defences at Kalith/Troti, suffering 41 killed and similar numbers injured.

Defences of Chhamb stood completely breached from two sides.

Enemy at Chhamb Temple which was desecrated

On the 5th itself 127 Div. Loc Battery radar section started to withdraw from Pt 994 as 5 Sikh had started to withdraw. 127 Div. Loc Battery came under attack by the enemy, very close to Chhamb Bridge, causing 10 casualties with multiple vehicles destroyed. The casualties were of driver L/Hav Karam Chand of a radar towing Kraz. He was also the first driver to young Second Lieutenant AK Kher in 1968. Upon joining the unit, Second Lieutenant Kher was taught how to drive by Karam

Chand. Hav Dila Ram was radar no. 1 (Operator Fire Control), Hav Kanshi Ram, Cook L/Nk Bakhshish Singh, who always wore a brand new uniform while cooking during practice camps and used to wax his moustache up, Gunner Ramu Kalabire, Chhagan Ram, Rajbir Singh, Chhaju Ram and two gunners, Praduman Singh and Ran Singh Yadav both of whom had cleared the Services Selection Board (SSB) and were due to go for officer's training were amongst those killed.

The radar-towing Kraz was on fire. In a show of tremendous courage, Captain Shrivastava, with the remaining troops, unhooked the radar from the burning Kraz and manually pushed it across the bridge to safety. Captain UC Shrivastava managed to save both the radars and took them safely to home banks.

The situation on the bridge was temporarily restored by elements of 81 Field Regiment, 12 Field, an Engineer company and Alpha Group of 9 Para SF.

Now on the 5th December 0400 hrs, all elements of the advancing 13 AK Battalion and some elements of 47 Punjab Battalion of the Pakistan Army managed to reach Mannawar Tawi at Mandiala crossing via the Sukhtau Nullah. Captain Mahajani, Adjutant of 216 Medium, reported troops in khaki crossing Mannawar Tawi to FDC. The Brigade Major Major Surya Narayan, divorced from the ground situation in the frontline and also from 191 Infantry Brigade HQ, warned him that perhaps the BSF troops were withdrawing and not to engage them. At 0430 hrs the full 13 AK Battalion with 47 Punjab of the enemy bumped into the forward batteries of 216 Medium Regiment.

Two forward batteries of 216 Medium were closest to Mannawar Tawi banks. The Marathas of 216 Medium were completely caught off guard, leading to confusion and a fierce close quarter hand-to-hand fighting with the Pakistanis ensued. The forward batteries of 216 Medium got disorganised. The depth Battery, however, engaged the two forward Battery locations in direct firing role and claimed 70 Pakistanis in the gun area but sadly 72 of 216 Medium boys also died with an additional 36 greviously wounded. As a ramification of this firing, a few guns of the forward Batteries were also damaged and both forward Batteries went out of action causing severe reduction in firepower to forward areas.

The Pakistanis bumping into 216 forward Batteries was purely accidental as the enemy was not carrying pole charges to destroy the guns.

Furthermore, the remaining elements of 13 AK Battalion and other elements of the enemy's 47 Punjab occupied the Kachrial Chaprial heights which was their primary objective. They were now engaging the gun positions of 39 Medium with observed small arms fire. Enemy Artillery OP on Kachrial Chaprial heights now had clear observation of the Northern and Southern Axis.

The loss of two Batteries of 216 Medium regiment caused immense desperation in forward OPs for saving their positions from being overrun by the enemy and further increased the pressure on 39 Medium to cover for reduction in firepower. There was so much demand from Laleali to Mannawar for defensive fire that at times one gun Battery of 39 Medium was shooting different targets over 100 degrees apart, at the same time.

There was also a time when the situation became so desperate that Captain RI Singh, OP at Laleali, could just be given only a single gun support to save his location and life.

68 Infantry Brigade's (ex Corp reserve) 7 Kumaon Rifles commanded by Lt Col Dahiya and 2IC Major Meer Fayazudin

were dispatched by the GOC 10 Div. along with a squadron of 72 Armoured Regiment as reinforcements from Akhnoor. They were tasked to evict the enemy from Kachrial Chaprial, counter attack Mandiala North and plug the gap between Mandiala and Buchomandi.

Meanwhile, the elements of 13 AK Battalion attacked the wagon line area of 39 Medium Regiment. 6 or 7 Non Combatant (NC'S E) of 39 Medium were killed in fierce brutal hand-to-hand combat. In the melee, driver Paramjit Singh's carbine jammed and the Pakistani JCO tried to bayonet him. Paramjit caught the enemy's rifle. The enemy tried to fire but it also was jammed. Paramjit was able to snatch the enemy JCO's rifle and killed him on the spot along with one more enemy soldier. Driver Paramjit Singh found a mention in dispatches for his valour.

Meanwhile, Major HS Dhinsa was the Battery Commander of 123 Med Battery. He was ex-Mule Artillery and a battle-hardened soldier from the 1965 war. Under his command, the Battery continued to provide fire support to forward areas in spite of the enemy being in the wagon lines and the gun area receiving considerable small arms' fire from Kachrial Chaprial heights.

To put an end to the nuisance of small arms fire, Major HS Dhinsa ordered turning of two guns towards Kachrial Chaprial heights and with open sights engaged the Pakistanis, using the guns in direct firing role. 37 Pakistanis lay dead and the rest ran back.

Major Dhinsa displayed tremendous courage, that of a tiger. Only visible were his two eyes, nose and mouth as the rest of his face was camouflaged by a thick black beard. The situation was stabilised near the 39 Medium gun area with the enemy retreating.

Meanwhile, 7 Kumaon Rifles was moving in vehicles along the Northern Axis from Akhnoor to counter attack Mandiala North. They had loaded their mortars along with ammunition in one-ton vehicles. Upon nearing Kachrial Chaprial heights, they got caught in the open and came under effective enemy Artillery fire. Their mortar carrying one-ton vehicles were destroyed and the mortar ammo started exploding, adding to the casualties. 7 Kumaon Rifles CO, along with four officers, one JCO and 42, were injured, two JCOs, Subedar Sree Krishna Joshi, N/Sub Hukum Singh and 19 ORs died, rendering the Battalion ineffective and no counter attack on Mandiala North could take place.

Two tanks of 72 Armoured Regiment appeared on the scene. They fired a couple of rounds towards Mandiala North. Thereafter they started going back and on enquiry by Major HS Dhinsa, informed that they would come back after refuelling. These tanks immediately came under enemy-observed Artillery bombardment, leading to Captain Mohan Lal Safaya getting killed.

7 Kumaon Rifles instead now occupied Buchomandi and Kachrial Chaprial heights, which by now were cleared of the enemy by the action of 39 Medium Regiment.

2IC of 13 AK Battalion, Major Abbasi was captured by a patrol party of 39 Medium. The Artillery OP officer of the Pakistanis, with 13 AK/47 Punjab Battalion, was also presumed killed and his walkie-talkie taken in by 39 Medium patrol party. Lt Col Bashrat Raja, CO of 13 AK Battalion was wounded and captured by L60 AD troop commander, Captain Kaul and immediately taken to Division HQ on 5th December itself for interrogation. The remaining surviving enemy elements retreated back across Mandiala crossing.

During this period, 39 Medium came under effective

enemy counter bombardment and Pakistani Air Force attack. This time its wagon lines were hit and a few vehicles destroyed, causing some casualties. Second Lieutenant Navnit Swaraj got hit by a splinter and was killed instantaneously in 39 Medium Gun area.

Captain PP Singh, 39 Medium's light repair workshop officer was instrumental in keeping the guns and vehicles in a serviceable state. In the enemy counter bombardment he was injured while carrying out repairs and was the only EME officer mentioned in dispatches for his courage.

In both conflicts, of 1965 and 1971, 39 Medium Regiment distinguished themselves. Older-generation soldiers in 39 used to say, "*Jethay ghamasan yudh hona 39 uddey Deploy ho ni.*" (Wherever there is a bloody war, 39 has to be deployed there.)

39 Medium Regiment in all lost three officers–Captain Ravinder Kaura, Captain AS Malik, Second Lieutenant Navnit Swaraj, two JCOs N/Sub Desa Singh and N/Sub Anant Singh and 30 other ranks were killed. Wounded were one officer, one JCO and 29 other ranks.

Desa Singh had a role in the 1965 operations too which is worth mentioning.

Haji Pir was an ingress route of infiltrators and its capture was vital as it controlled the old Mughal Road to Kashmir. All artillery fire was ineffective capturing it as the target was out of range. Guns could not be moved forward due to non-existent roads and a very difficult mountainous terrain laid restrictions on forward deployment.

The Khalsas, under the leadership of Lieutenant GS Sandhu, Gun Position Officer (GPO) dismantled two guns on Nund Singh bridge in Uri and loaded them on one-ton and moved forward across the CFL to village Khoza Bandi. The guns were assembled on the road itself as no gun area existed.

They then fired with charge super but still the shells were landing short of the target. Under orders of Lieutenant Sandhu, the Khalsas added a few more increment charges to charge super (not allowed as the gun may burst, killing the detachment).

Disregarding the risk and after a loud Khalsa war cry, they fired the shells which this time landed on the target.

Desa Singh kept on firing till Haji Pir was captured. At that moment only four Medium Guns of–

Gun Detachment in URI 1965

122 Battery were deployed in Uri/Baramulla in troop strength supporting 5 Infantry Battalions with the arc of fire being over 200 degrees. At times all four guns fired in different centres of arc.

Captain Sultan Mahmood was Battery Commander Medium Troop in Kashmir. The issue of *Illustrated Weekly* 1965 showed a 5.5 inch gun in action firing for the Haji Pir attack by 1 Para SF Batallion led by Major Ranjit Singh Dyal

MVC, who later went on to become Army Commander.

But this time N/Sub Desa Singh got a direct hit from a Pakistani shell and only a few bits of his body could be found for performing the last rites.

After the debacle on the banks of Mannawar Tawi gun area, Depth Battery of 216 Medium withdrew to an area 2 or 3 km east of Pahari Wala on the Northern Axis and was the only battery of 216 Medium which was in action and firing effectively.

Enemy Artillery Fire

The Enemy fired about 1 lakh rounds of ammunition on our BOPs and defences on 3rd December night, as per the captured fire plan of the Pakistani OP officer. The Artillery available to Pakistan was two Batteries of 17 pounder guns, two 25 pounder regiments, two 122 mm howitzer regiments, one 105 mm howitzer regiment, two 155 mm howitzer regiments, one composite regiment with a mix of 105 mm and 3.7 inch howitzers.

Fire was accurate and observed, as the enemy had clear information about our dispositions and had effectively infiltrated their commando OPs in our territory prior to the war. The effect of this bombardment on our forward troops was paralysing.

Demise of Lt Col AB Guha, CO of 12 Field Regiment

Lt Col AB Guha, the CO of 12 Field, was very soft-spoken and a diehard gunner. On the fateful day of 5th December he was wearing a DR leather jacket without sleeves over his jersey and travelling with Subedar Major (SM) of 216 Medium for redeploying guns. They came under Pakistani air attack. On sighting the enemy aircraft, they got down from the jeep and stood by the roadside. Lt Col Guha, instead of himself taking cover, told his driver, "*Arre bhai tum kyo marta hai, position lay lo*." A 500 pounder directly landed on him and he, along with Subedar Major Datta Ram Shindolkar, was blown away.

Field Artillery Situation on 5/6th December 1971

18 Field Regiment Battery, two Batteries of 12 Field Regiment and 81 Field started to withdraw to depth positions in Pallanwala area on the home side of the river. One gun of 81 Field Regiment, which was damaged due to a direct hit on the 4th December morning, was also taken back to main defences.

L/Nk Shinde, a tractor driver of 81 Field and a courageous soldier, while withdrawing, encountered some enemy troops, who tried to stop him but he charged them and drove off amidst a hail of small arms fire, saving the gun from falling into enemy hands.

Artillery Fire Direction Centre (FDC) also withdrew to area Khore in Pallanwala.

Bold use of slow-moving T-6G trainer aircraft with 0.30 (7.62 mm) machine gun was deployed by the Pakistanis for strafing our withdrawing forces from 5th December onwards. This aircraft was active on Southern Axis near area Khore as there was no Air Defence (AD) cover.

While withdrawing from Chhamb, Captain AK Kher and his troops came under fire from this aircraft at Khore Crossing on Lokhi Khad. One of his troop's one-ton with FDC equipment got bogged down in slush and all means employed to extricate it failed. Due to fear of fire from the enemy aircraft, no heavy vehicle stopped to help until a passing three-ton was forcibly stopped at gun point and the driver threatened by Captain Kher.

The tow chain from one-ton was attached to the three-ton and the one-ton was successfully pulled out while the enemy aircraft was making multiple passes and firing. As luck would have it, nobody got hit!

This aircraft was finally hit by Indian ground fire after causing considerable nuisance, but it managed to cross back to Pakistan.

Due to the debacle of 5 Assam and the enemy infiltrating via Sukhtau Nullah in the 5 Sikh location, 191 Infantry Brigade had no alternative left apart from withdrawing. The withdrawal was organised and militarily coordinated. Nobody ran back to rear areas. Pakistani forces didn't immediately pursue the withdrawing Indians and now the entire 191 Infantry Brigade and field guns in reasonable shape were on the home side of Mannawar Tawi, to be deployed in depth areas.

Enemy at Chhamb Village

Final Situation in 28 Brigade Sector

The Pakistani assault on the Northern Axis was totally destroyed by the action of 39 Medium Regiment and this greatly stabilised the situation in 10 Infantry Division sector.

Situation in 52 Brigade Sector

There was some Pakistani action in 10 Garhwal unit areas Raipur and Darh crossing (part of 191 Inf Brigade) which was effectively dealt with by Defensive Fire (DF) and company-level local counter attacks. Sangam Post and 15 Alpha were captured by the enemy.

In this sector, Pakistan had employed Sherman tanks which were obsolete and ineffective. Except for a few enemy provocations, there was not much action in this sector. The enemy formed up a few times in front of 16 Punjab in Thako Chak area, but no assault was delivered and the status quo was maintained.

□

9

Counter Attack

On 5th December, after the enemy had captured Pt 994 in 5 Sikh location, Major General Jaswant Singh decided to withdraw to Kalith, Troti and Dhon Chak main defensive areas.

On 5th/6th December Lt General Sartaj Singh, the Corps Commander ordered the 10 Infantry Division Commander to carry adjustments to the defences to contain the advancing enemy. He introduced all elements of reserve 68 Infantry Brigade into battle as the new front line was emerging at Raipur Crossing, Darh Crossing (Dud), Mandiala Crossing and from Buchomandi to Nathuan Tibba, Dewa waterpoint, Laleali, Pt 707 and Kalidhar.

On 5th/6th December, 9 JAT, commanded by Lt Col Jagjit Singh, with two squadrons of 72 Armoured was deployed on the east side of Mannawar Tawi, around Darh and Raipur Crossing.

5/8 Gorkha was positioned east of Mandiala Bridge to stop the enemy onslaught and with one platoon of 5 Sikh and two tank troop of 9 Deccan Horse was tasked to counter attack Mandiala. Upon commencement of counter attack, 5/8 Gorkha found they were completely unfamiliar with the terrain and took a few casualties, making the counter attack ineffective. 5/8 Gorkha lost Second Lieutenant PR Sharma and two ORs.

By 6th December, the enemy had captured Gogi, Barsala and Singri area after persistent attacks and reached the banks of the Mannawar Tawi on the southwest side. 4/1 Gorkha had vacated Chak Pandit and Malkay Camp. The situation became precarious when 9 Deccan Horse and 72 Armour Regiment, instead of counter attacking, started taking layback positions at this critical stage.

The Pakistani armour was now trying to cross Mannawar Tawi at Darh Crossing and Raipur Crossing. The enemy was trying to gain a bridge head in the area after successfully penetrating Mandiala Crossing earlier causing havoc in 216 Medium Forward Gun area.

7 Garhwal, commanded by Lt Col Rana of 52 Infantry Brigade, was moved from Pallanwala area to hold ground at Nathu Kulian, the area opposite Chatti Tali and the area opposite Sangam Post to defend against the enemy onslaught.

Finally, the eastern part of Chhamb Bridge was demolished by engineers after complete withdrawal close to midnight of 6th December, 1971, while beefing up the defences on the home side of the river line.

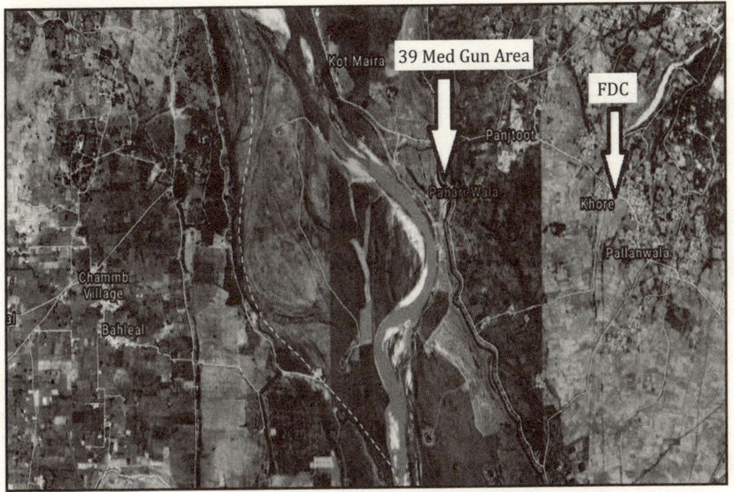

Location of 39 Medium Regiment and FDC (Google Maps)

39 Medium Regiment also withdrew from Kachrial Chaprial area and redeployed at Pahari Wala gun area between 6th and 7th December. The guns were deployed in a natural dry *nallah*, giving supporting fire to the whole 10 Div. Sector.

From 7th December onwards, the IAF was pressed into serious ground support role in Chhamb to hold the enemy back from advancing further.

Pakistani Assault Across Mannawar Tawi

The situation now became even more dangerous as the enemy broke through 9 JAT deployed at Darh Crossing. This area had heavy *sarkanda* growth and 9 JAT was not patrolling the water line nor had they posted observation. They were caught totally by surprise by the swift, ruthless Pakistani assault. 9 JAT suffered heavy casualties with Company Commander Major SC Guleri, who had just got married on 22nd October, 1971 and been recalled back to the unit within four days of marriage, presumed killed and Second Lieutenant RM Naresh confirmed killed. The enemy got a foothold across the water line. Captain Kher had met Major SC Guleri in November at Akhnoor concentration area and had taken lunch with his company.

On the 7th December night, the enemy attacked Raipur Crossing defended by Major Hardev Singh Grewal's company and was repulsed a number of times, but enemy regrouped and persisted with the attack. Major Hardev was killed on 9th December, fighting valiantly and was awarded the VrC. The enemy was also able to overrun and disperse two platoon locations of 10 Garhwal and now had taken both Darh and Raipur Crossing and had a reasonable lodgment east of Mannawar Tawi (home side).

IAF raid on 39 Medium Regiment

On 9th December, approximately at 1400 hrs, the bomb line given to IAF in panic was west of Lauki Khad. IAF's strike package of 5 SU-7 (ground attack) and two MiG 21 (combat air patrol) mistook 39 Medium Gun Area as an enemy position and first strafed and then further went on to drop a 1000-pounder on 39 Medium Regiment location which was well deployed on home side around 4 kms away from Lauki Khad dry *nallah* area. In this friendly fire, nine ORs of 39 Medium were killed including the EME N/Sub. Two Kraz gun-towers loaded with ammo and a *gurudwara* vehicle was blown up. The unit *Granthi* was grievously wounded.

The CO 39 Medium Lt Col Gauri Shankar had to order the AD Battery to fire at the IAF on their second bomb run to deter them from further action.

Meanwhile, all efforts were being made to extricate guns damaged/disabled in 216 Medium forward gun areas in Chaprial the previous gun area. On the fateful night of 9th December, Lt Col ML Sethi, CO of 216 Medium Regiment, was himself evacuating damaged guns via the Northern Axis. He came under effective small arms fire of own troops (Field Bty deployed in the area) and was killed. This unfortunate incident could have been the result of confusion caused by battle fatigue.

It is pertinent to mention here that Lt Col ML Sethi had taken command of 216 Medium Regiment at Chandi Mandir just before deployment. He earlier commanded 18 Field Regiment at Jaurian, the neighbouring unit of Captain Kher's 127 Div. Loc Battery.

On 10th December 1971, the Corps Commander Lt General Sartaj Singh, with his GSO-1 Col Mahinder Singh, drove to FDC Khore and bellowed to Henry, Commander 10 Artillery

Brigade, "Get into my jeep." Brigadier Henry Srinivasan started picking up his maps upon which he was told, "I know this area like the back of my hand, Henry, just come with me," and they drove to the area Darh Crossing.

Lt General Sartaj Singh assumed command and countermanded all withdrawal orders, "You bastards, no running back; stay put where you are." And this was personally heard by Captain Kher.

Lt General Sartaj ordered Brigadier Trevor Morlin commanding 68 Infantry Brigade (ex-Corps Reserve) with remaining elements of 9 JAT, 7 Kumaon, 5/8 Gorkha, 10 Garhwal (191 Infantry Brigade) and 3 /4 Gorkha (52 Infantry Brigade), 9 Deccan Horse and 72 Armour Regiment to now counter attack Chhamb. Brigadier Trevor instead told him that he would first stabilise the eastern banks of Mannawar Tawi.

Artillery fire plan VINOD was organised for the counter attack on the Darh-Raipur lodgment of the enemy in support of 68 Infantry Brigade counter attack. A total of 5,000 rounds of Artillery ammunition was fired to cover this attack, to soften the enemy lodgements.

Two companies of 3/4 Gorkha with support of Deccan Horse counter attacked Darh Crossing from the north. The Armour generally got bogged down but the water line was recaptured and occupied after a fierce battle. 3/4 Gorkha lost three officers Major VK Behl, Major Vijendra Singh, Captain HK Mehta and a JCO N/Sub Madan Singh Gurung.

Two companies of 10 Garhwal, led by Lt Col Onkar Singh and Major Mahabir Negi supported by 72 Armour, attacked from the south and captured Raipur Crossing, which the enemy had already vacated. Lt Col Onkar Singh was unfortunately critically wounded with a stray bullet hitting him in the stomach in this counter attack and he later succumbed to his injuries.

It was presumed that the enemy withdrew due to a vacuum created in Pakistani leadership by Major General Iftikar's chopper being shot down by our forces on 9th December. He was coordinating and positioning his troops over Chhamb and was critically wounded and subsequently died on the 10th December, 1971. His successor did not have the same resolve as Major General Iftikar to hold the bridgehead and instead focused on consolidating the captured eastern banks of Mannawar Tawi.

One T59 Pakistani tank lay on our side of the water line and its turret and gun were 20 metres away from the main body of the tank, presumably destroyed by a medium shell. No enemy dead bodies were seen as the enemy had evacuated and this was observed by Captain AK Kher who was flying with Air OP. This enemy tank is at PDC location at Armoured Regiment gates to date.

Alfa Commando Group of Major Ashok Cariappa

After withdrawal and loss of Chhamb, Para Commandos of 9 Para SF went into Pakistan-occupied Chhamb to doing exactly what they trained for – to spread panic and cause destruction beyond enemy lines. Lieutenant SN Singh of 39 Medium was the Artillery OP officer with this commando group for covert action and had taken part in three or four such raids. He took shots, causing damage to the enemy. A few B Echlon vehicles in the Gopar area were destroyed with some enemy casualties and an enemy tank in Nadala area was hit with a rocket launcher by the commandos.

Alpha Group also suffered the loss of Nk Ram Singh, Nk Hoshiar Singh and L/Nk Om Prakash and 14 wounded, over the number of days of battle. Captain MA Cariappa was awarded the Sena Medal for bravery in saving the Chhamb

Bridge during the initial assault by the enemy and yes there were two Cariappas in the Alpha Group.

The Forces on both sides were in a holding pattern from 10th December onwards and no effective counter attack was carried out by 10 Infantry Division to recover the enemy-captured areas west of Tawi even though there was a massive reserve force available to the Corps Commander.

On 12th December, a reconnaissance patrol led by Second Lieutenant Nagarjun Sisodia of 3/4 Gorkha was ambushed and grievously wounded as there were some stray enemy elements still lurking around in the area. The patrol made it back to the unit but sadly Second Lieutenant Sisodia succumbed to his injuries on 13th December.

In 52 Brigade sector on 14th December, 16 Punjab was ordered to launch an attack in Thako Chak area which ended in a disaster as all the observations related to Pakistani positions, well defended by company strength of force and a tank troop, were disregarded by the higherups.

At the preparatory stage itself the enemy had observed 16 Punjab marking their FUP (Forming up Positions) and direction markers. The Pakistanis had suitably deployed two MMGs on trees to cover the area of assault effectively. Once the attack developed at an appropriate time, the Pakistani MMGs opened up from the trees and massacred the assaulting troops. 16 Punjab had one JCO N/Sub Tarsem Singh and 19 other ranks killed and 20 wounded in one single operation. Captain Bahadur, who was one of the injured, was a company mate of Captain Kher from OTS.

Subsequently there was no further offensive action in 16 Punjab sector. This attack operation order was converted into a raid on paper to protect personalities on our side.

A sudden ceasefire was announced on the 16th December, 1971.

Just as the ceasefire rolled in on 17th December, 1971, 10 Garhwal position was engaged by the enemy from Nathu Kulian from across the river. 10 Garhwal, however, attacked and captured Nathu Kulia.

Sangam Post in 52 Infantry Brigade sector, was attacked and recaptured by 7 Garhwal's Major Sharawat. The attack was supported by Artillery Brigade. On this night, 11 guns of 216 Medium Regiment were in action and took part in a fire plan to capture Sangam Post.

15 Alpha Post was also recaptured as the enemy had moved back to its main defences.

Enemy Air Action

The initial three days of war saw Pakistan Air Force (PAF) in a very active mode. Six to seven Sabers would come at a time and unload their ammo on Indian positions. Mostly medium gun areas were the target.

Accuracy in air attack was deterred by the presence of AD Battery in the area. However, the PAF still managed to destroy many gun-tower vehicles. The POL Dump (Petrol Oil and Lubricant) at Jaurian was bombed and it was lost to fire.

The Ammunition point in Akhnoor on Sundarbani Road was also bombed and tank ammunition of 100 mm calibre was destroyed along with other ammo.

IAF Action

On 4th December morning, around 0915 hrs, a mission of 2 SU-7 aircraft flew over Chhamb to attack the enemy positions in ground support role, but unfortunately one SU-7 was shot down by the enemy's AA fire. The pilot bailed over our own area in Burejal and was rescued.

It was later found that the pilot was Flight Lieutenant Gurdip Singh of 101 Squadron, operating from Adampur. For the next three days, there was no sign of IAF over Chhamb.

Only after four days of battle did the IAF establish air supremacy and the PAF vanished from the sky. It was now only the IAF flying from Pathankot and Adampur airbases.

On 8th December, an IAF MiG 21 was brought down by Pakistani AD guns. The pilot bailed out over our territory south of Chhamb. It was later confirmed to be Squadron Leader Denzil Keelor of 1965 fame and he was rescued.

MiG 21 brought down by enemy's ground fire on 8th December 1971

IAF raid on enemy gun positions

Locating Battery had given the location of the enemy's Medium Gun positioned at Burejal. Brigade Major Major Surya Narayan ordered AK Kher to organise an illuminated marker to point the direction of Burejal from ALG Khore.

On Captain Kher's instructions, BHM Bhawar Singh produced 40 hurricane lamps from abandoned villages, painted black on enemy side and made an arrow to indicate the exact direction. By midnight, the Canberra bombers came and aligning with the arrow bombed Burejal. Continuous fire and explosions were observed, indicating heavy enemy damages in the Burejal area.

The SU-7 was a big aircraft; the enemy used their MMGs and LMGs effectively against it. Group Captain Dandekar, on his visit to 39 Medium Mess after the operations ended, said that every SU that came over Chhamb, returned with bullet holes.

AOC (Air Officer Commanding) of Pathankot was Gp Captain MS Dandekar and of Adampur was Gp Captain Randhir Singh.

□

10

The Ceasefire

At 2000 hrs on 16th December, 1971, a ceasefire was declared.

The Pakistani offensive and the operations were halted on the river line Mannawar Tawi, with Chhamb lost to Pakistan.

The Pakistanis could not advance beyond Chhamb to capture Akhnoor and choke communication lines between Jammu & Kashmir and the rest of India as was their main objective of war.

The grand design of Pakistan to capture Akhnoor Bridge was squarely defeated.

India suffered the maximum casualties of the 1971 war in the battle of Chhamb.

We totaled approximately 500 killed; out of this, more than a 100 were gunners, 723 wounded and 190 missing or Prisoners of War.

On ceasefire night, eleven guns of 216 Medium were in action; the damaged guns of 216 Medium on Mannawar Tawi banks were recovered and moved to the workshop.

One gun of 81 Field at Sakrana was damaged and was evacuated to the rear. No gun of 86 Light, 18 Field, 12 Field or 39 Medium was damaged by enemy action.

Eighteen tanks and a number of vehicles and other equipment were lost.

Own Artillery Ammo Expenditure

In the entire battle of Chhamb, the Artillery ammunition expended was about 77,000 rounds, 39 Medium Regiment fired about 17,000 rounds which is 34 second-line ammo, 81 Field fired about 6,400 rounds, 86 Light fired 1,300 rounds of mortar ammo and the rest of the ammo was fired by 12 Field,18 Field and 216 Medium Regiment.

Inferences

Pakistan repeated the textbook 1965 war plan in 1971 exactly.

In November itself, there were enough indications that Pakistan was preparing for an attack.

On 1st December their armour assembled in forward areas and this was taken lightly by Div. Commander.

191 Infantry Brigade continued to remain in firm base for facilitating an attack by 68 Infantry Brigade on Pakistan. The defences were not readjusted upon receiving the enemy-attack intelligence. The gap in 5 Assam defences was not plugged. The dummy minefield was not mined.

At a crucial time, the GOC positioned at Pallanwala TAC HQ was without command control setup and could not influence the battle.

There was no counter attack at Division level.

10 Infantry Division didn't effectively plug the gaps and were caught offbalance between offensive and defence action.

India lost about 120 sq km area.

A New Ceasefire Line was drawn after 1971.

39 Medium War Memorial

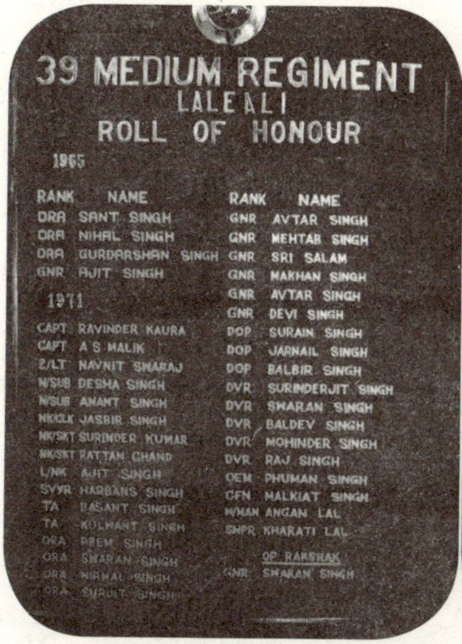

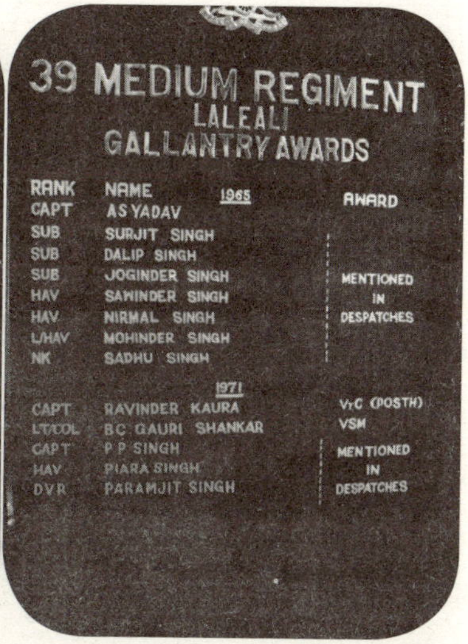

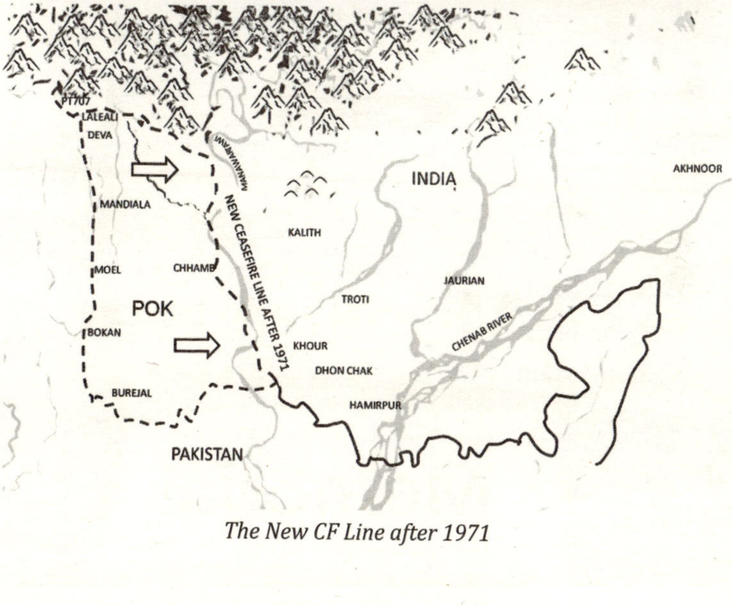

39 MEDIUM REGIMENT
LALEALI
ROLL OF HONOUR

1965

RANK NAME
DRA SANT SINGH
DRA NIHAL SINGH
DRA GURDARSHAN SINGH
GNR AJIT SINGH

1971

CAPT RAVINDER KAURA
CAPT A S MALIK
2/LT NAVNIT SHARAJ
N/SUB DESHA SINGH
N/SUB ANANT SINGH
NK/CLK JASBIR SINGH
NK/SKT SURINDER KUMAR
NK/SKT RATTAN CHAND
L/NK AJIT SINGH
SVYR HARBANS SINGH
TA BASANT SINGH
TA KULWANT SINGH
ORA PREM SINGH
ORA SWARAN SINGH
ORA NIRMAL SINGH
ORA SURJIT SINGH

RANK NAME
GNR AVTAR SINGH
GNR MEHTAB SINGH
GNR SRI SALAM
GNR MAKHAN SINGH
GNR AVTAR SINGH
GNR DEVI SINGH
DOP SURAIN SINGH
DOP JARNAIL SINGH
DOP BALBIR SINGH
DVR SURINDERJIT SINGH
DVR SWARAN SINGH
DVR BALDEV SINGH
DVR MOHINDER SINGH
DVR RAJ SINGH
OEM PHUMAN SINGH
CFN MALKIAT SINGH
W/MAN ANGAN LAL
SMPR KHARATI LAL

OP RAKSHAK
GNR SWARAN SINGH

39 MEDIUM REGIMENT
LALEALI
GALLANTRY AWARDS

RANK	NAME	AWARD
	1965	
CAPT	AS YADAV	
SUB	SURJIT SINGH	MENTIONED IN DESPATCHES
SUB	DALIP SINGH	
SUB	JOGINDER SINGH	
HAV	SAWINDER SINGH	
HAV	NIRMAL SINGH	
L/HAV	MOHINDER SINGH	
NK	SADHU SINGH	
	1971	
CAPT	RAVINDER KAURA	VrC (POSTH)
LT/COL	B C GAURI SHANKAR	VSM
CAPT	P P SINGH	MENTIONED IN DESPATCHES
HAV	PIARA SINGH	
DVR	PARAMJIT SINGH	

The New CF Line after 1971

Comrades taken POW by the Pakistanis in Chhamb and some still languishing in enemy prisons till date

1. 5 Sikh
2. 4/1 Gorkha
3. 16 Punjab
4. 81 Field Arty
5. 5 Assam

□

11

Post Ceasefire

Major Rajinder Singh, Company Commander 4/1 Gorkha, who was deployed at Jhanda, personally came to Pahari Wala gun area of 39 Medium after the operations ended and hugged each and every Gun No 1. He thanked Captain SN Singh (who had picked up his rank) and all gunners of 123 Medium Battery for saving his company with timely and accurate fire support and with tears in his eyes he told all the No. 1s, "I cannot give you decorations but from my side each one of you deserves an MVC."

After complete redrawing of the India-Pakistan border in this sector following the ceasefire, 39 Medium Regiment was moved to Akhnoor area for rest and refit.

Captain AK Kher officially joined 39 Medium Regiment a day after the ceasefire.

Hav Nirmal Singh, an ace gunner and a detachment commander, was an unassuming and humorous guy of the regiment. Every year on Raising Day, he would read a newsletter on badaa Khaana.

The newsletter was usually about the happenings in the regiment for the past year and it used to be a standup comedy in the original form. Hav Nirmal Singh, at the first badaa Khaana after the war, broke out the news about Captain AK Kher joining the unit as follows:

"*Yeh* Radio 39 *hai, hamare yaha bade der ka bad ik tagda officer aya hai paar ik zabardust problem hai ki isko kahan camouflage karen*?" (39 officers except CO were lean and average built but Kher was big built and the units were still operating under camouflage nets).

Nissan One-Ton

39 Medium had world II vintage one-ton vehicles. On the road to Akhnoor, it was a common sight to see many one-tons stranded and frustrated drivers making efforts at starting them.

On one occasion, a Sardarji's one-ton was stuck on the road. With the bonnet up, his turban back to front, sleeves rolled up, a bottle of petrol in one hand and a rubber tube in the other, he was working on it.

On seeing this, while driving down the road, the Commander of 10 Artillery Brigade, Henry Srinivasan was curious. He stopped and looked. It turned out to be a 39 Medium Singh's vehicle.

"Kya ho raha hai Jawan?" (What is happening, soldier?)"

"Sahibji, yey government nay manu keho ji gadi deti ha jadu petrol nahi honda, bottal nal carborater che petrol panda,

fer overflow hondi tay pipe nal kud lan da, do ghanta ho gaye chalan da nam nahi landi."

(What kind of vehicle has the government given me? Petrol does not go into carburetor and I have to manually pour it and then it overflows and then I try to take it out by pipe. It's been two hours but this damn vehicle refuses to start). On hearing this, the Commander quietly left the scene.

In early summer of 1972, Lt Col Gauri Shankar got posted out to TAC Wing School of Artillery, Devlali after an eventful command from 12th May, 1969 and Lt Col AS Rathore took over command of the unit in Akhnoor area on 15th May, 1972.

Farewell of Lt Col Gauri Shankar from the Unit

122 Medium Battery was ordered to move to Krishna Ghati and Bimber Gali area to support 25 Infantry Division as they didn't have medium gun support.

While moving on Sundarbani Hills, L/Nk Paramjit Singh, the driver who had killed two enemy combatants in hand-to-hand combat, while driving was not able to negotiate a sharp turn with his gun-towing Kraz and went straight down 500 feet into the *nallah*. The gun was recovered and suffered minor damages and was repaired, but the Kraz was a total writeoff and sadly L/Nk Paramjit Singh, along with a Jawan, did not make it through.

After a few months, the remaining two Batterys of 39 Medium Regiment were also ordered to move to 25 Infantry Division sector in Nowshera area with Regimental HQ at Talay Camp. 393 Medium Battery was deployed at Chetya Kabra/ Kongata and 123 Medium Battery at Dhral.

The driver of gun tower, L/Nk Gurcharan Singh (Buda) of 123 Medium Battery of Mattewala action fame, met with an accident too. On a hilly bend his Kraz with gun went off the road and over a hut, demolishing it and inflicting some casualties on the people inside.

Captain Kher, upon reaching the spot, enquired, *"Aay, kinda hoya Gurcharana*?"

(How did this happen, Gurcharan?)

Gurcharan, *"Sahib, maa steering takat nal fade see, aa makan tey uthou tay, appa he lung gayee*." (I had held the steering wheel with power but the Kraz on its own went over the hut.)

Captain Kher suspected problems with Gurcharan's eyesight and an eye test was ordered. Eyesight tests confirmed that he was partially blind and not fit to drive.

Now who would explain this to brave Gurcharan? Spectacles were made for him but unfortunately he never wore them.

"Loke mazaq karda, saaza daou, chashma nahin pehna," said Gurcharan.

(People make fun of me. Punish me but Gurcharan will not wear spectacles.)

While deploying guns at night, when only the side lights were to be used, all gun towers came in action, using only the side lights.

Gurcharan's gun also came in action flawlessly but without any lights at all in pitch darkness, so it was concluded Gurcharan *dil thee roshni nal kraz chalonda*. (He drives with sight and light emitting from his heart.)

A few months later, a military exercise was held to consolidate the positions on the border. Major Dhinsa and Captain Kher were on reconnaissance in a remote border area. A suspicious-looking civilian waved to them seeking a lift. Major Dhinsa asked the driver to stop and told the civilian, "*Aa jaa, bay jaa; par meri ik sharat hai; iss gaddi chi baithan vastay government jitnee mary bund marti ha bus ooda 5% tu manu marna dey*." Second time, while they again were on recon, a civilian was looking and following them constantly, maybe just out of curiosity or maybe there was more to it but for sure he was an undesirable in the area.

Major Dhinsa stopped and shouted, "*Oye, tu ki lena, lunn layna, aaja mera fud laa*." The character got the message that they were on to him and he was not seen thereafter. Major Dhinsa had received intelligence that the area had some undesirable elements from across the border and they had to be alert about that.

After successful deployment, Major Dhinsa was pleased as there were no undersirable incidents and announced a single Rum issue for men. One issue of rum was the limit as consuming beyond that meant the men's alertness would have fallen and tensions were still high on the border. Tents were pitched and all the men were sitting outside their tents. The Major was a little away, drying his hair and mane as after a long hiatus he had the opportunity to wash up.

Papa Gurmit was the Battery Dispatch Rider (DR) Captain Kher's usual driver was on leave so Papa was driving his jeep. He came to Captain Kher and threw a smart salute, "*Sahibji, suna hai ajj rum issue hai.*" Captain Kher said, "Jes!" "Sahibji, mera ik peg naal kucch naye banda. Manu dooja peg chayeda." (One drink is not enough, I need two.)

Captain Kher said, "*Papa, meri authority ik peg thee hai. Jey tanu doojha peg chayeda to badday sardar nu salute mar.*" (Major Dhinsa was within earshot of the conversation.)

Papa went to Battery Commander, saluted and requested for an extra peg.

Major Dhinsa, "*Papa tu manu dus, maa tanu duja peg kyon divan? Tu mera keda extra lunfuud ta? Duja peg chyda toh aaaza, onu fud la.*" Papa Gurmit ran for his life.

Once upon a time there was a Sikh warrior and he was Santokh Singh

A few months later, Captain AK Kher was posted OP officer at Pir Budeshwar (PB), which was a ground of tactical importance in 120 Infantry Brigade sector with his OP party. The usual OP party rotation was about two to three months at a time. PB was the highest post in the area and was about 5,500 feet above sea level. It was a dominating feature overlooking the entire Khuriatta valley by observation and on a good day, especially after the showers, even the lights of Mangla Dam in Mirpur were visible, which was about 40 kms away. Govind Garh Fort, deep in Pakistan, was also visible from this spot.

The post top and the spurs covering the approaches were defended by one Infantry Company of 7 Mahar Regiment commanded by Major Swinder Singh. The CO of the 7 Mahar Unit was Lt Col Mangat Singh.

The post was graced by an ancient temple and there was a natural spring with plenty of fresh water about a fifteen minute walk down from it.

After a few days on the post, Captain Kher said to Santok Singh, "MC/BC my health going down, food bad, your ADM bakwas." Santok Singh, "*Sahib, post is isolated nayda they tadey, kucch nahin hi, bannay ka uppar gujjar ki bast hai, ana jana doo ghante lagta hai. Maharis khende daay hai, raising day per hi good food milega.*"(The post is isolated, right, left, nothing available. On the border there is a Gujjar hamlet. Going to and fro is about two hours' walk; the Mahars have said good food will be only available on Raising Day.)After a few days, Captain Kher started getting fresh milk with breakfast and a good amount of curd served during lunch. But Mahars, who were responsible for the *langar*, were dependent on milk powder and only when a bigger potato visited the post, would they be served tea with Milkmaid milk. Getting fresh milk from Supply was a distant dream.

Captain Kher, "Oye Santokh, mera welfare ab theekthak hai. How come fresh milk?" Santok Singh, after tweaking his moustache, "*Ai sadda kaam hai, apne sahib di dekh-bhal karna.*"(Our job is to take care of you.)

Captain Kher, after sustained enquiry, learned that Santokh would go out on line-check every day. He searched around for milk and found a source at about one hour's walking distance away from the post in Gujjar *basti* located near the border. The story goes thus: Santok to Gujjar, "*Oye gujjar, tere kol doodh hai*?" Gujjar, "*Sardarji, nahin idhar doodh kitthey*?" Santok, "*Oye saley, tere 2 bansay momay full, tu kenda ki doodh nahin hai.*" Gujjar, "*Nahin hi sardarji.*" Santok enraged, took out a loaded magazine, cocked his SLR and said, "*Saley bole tere kol doodh hai*?" Gujjar, "Haanji, Sardarji, doodh hai." Santok,

"*Kitnee ma killo*?" Gujjar, "Sardarji sava rupiey." Santok, now raising his SLR, "Foodey ki, bole 8 anna killo." Gujjar, "Sardarji, 8 anna killo." Santok, now pleased, "Okay half distance you bring, half distance I come and before delivery, Gujjar, you will drink four sips in front of me," and this is how Santok managed the milk for his officer.

Captain Kher's bunker telephone was a parallel line with OP post telephone. Santok Singh was on observation duty and Major Singh was at gun position, Dhral.

Santok to Major, "Hellow 43, all well?" 43 to 45 (OP), "All well, CO Sahib happy, moral high, today double issue." Santok, "*Oye Mejara, assi sukhey baithe hain idher.*"

Major, "*Keei hoya*?" Santok, "Not even one drop; Mahar company soldiers tell us to wait for Raising Day, only then we will have an issue of rum." Major, "*Chal koyee gal nahin, maa pitiyaa tu pittee eko gal hi.*"

Santok, "*Majora, telephone ma phook maar.*" Major, "Phook." Santok, "*Ahh, mazaa aya, khushboo aagayee, ik baari aur maar.*" Major, "*Phook*!."

Santok, "*Ah mazaa aya*. Thank you, Major," Captain Kher was listening to all this on the parallel phone line and decided to have a laugh and keep shut.

MT Hav Mukthar Singh

Mukthar the Great was a big *zamindar* (landlord) and an efficient and effective man. One day he came to Captain Kher's room and sought permission to give a vehicle battery to the CHM (Company Havaldar Major) of the EME workshop. Captain Kher was perplexed and asked how could he do that and why would he even do it?

He explained, "*Battery ka total ma pura kar langa* (I will take care of the inventory total). This CHM is an important man in the workshop as he can sign BLR (beyond local repair) certificate. On handing taking over with the other unit, we need his help." Move orders for the unit had already been received.

Captain Kher, after a thought relented. Mukthar further asked for a *chit* (bottle) too.

Mukthar arranged a chicken and gave a good party to the CHM EME; he even sent two men with the vehicle battery and escorted him back to the workshop, which was a mile away through a jungle.

Usually in handing or taking over, Singhs are very bad in accounting. They believe in trust but the Quarter Master branch believed in correct protocol. The Singhs would declare unusable stores and spares as BLR and deposit them with the Quarter Master (QM). Then these Khalsas would not file the deposit vouchers correctly, ultimately causing huge losses. The BLR stores had to be deposited in salvage depot and based on this voucher only, a new item could be requisitioned.

As we had no items on ground here, the CHM EME would come in and sign anything for Mukthar, to clear the loss. The reason for Mukthar to give the battery was that CHM EME had damaged a battery in the workshop. His OC was insisting on making him pay for it and this was Mukthar's way to help him when in need.

Mohinder Singh Dardi

This incident from the 1965 operations is worth mentioning as this constitutes Captain Kher's Battery history. Mohinder Singh was a white-skinned, handsome, blue-eyed, brave Sardar. He was the driver of a special vehicle at the Chhamb sector in 1965.

Back then in the 1965 war, 39 Medium Regiment had only two Batteries, namely 122 and 123. The regiment was deployed all over Jammu & Kashmir. Four guns of 122 Battery were at Uri, supporting the attack on the Haji Pir Pass. One gun was in Krishna Gati, one in Bimber Gali and 123 Medium Battery was in Chhamb sector. The Regimental HQ was at Sunderbani, which was away from both the Batteries and had little influence over the battle. Lt Col PS Siddhu commanded the unit.

Chhamb came under heavy enemy attack with 90 tanks and one division of Infantry. India had only one squadron of AMX 13 tanks of the 20 Lancers, who fought bravely against a far-superior enemy but were outflanked, outgunned and outnumbered. Major Bhaskar Roy of 20 Lancers was leading the AMX squadron and was killed.

The Pakistani Army made outflanking moves and the Indian troops were trapped. One Artillery regiment lost its guns and the Infantry units got dispersed. Despite this, 123 Medium Battery gave hell to the enemy tanks as medium guns were a potent weapon against them.

Two 39 Medium Regiment officers were injured in enemy bombardment and one officer Second Lieutenant RI Singh, who was wounded while fighting and taken POW. There was no officer left in the gun area.

Due to outflanking by the enemy tanks, many units fell back through 39 Medium gun area.

And now 39 gun positions had become vulnerable to the enemy. Drivers were ordered to get gun towers for hooking up the guns, but the MACK trucks would not start as the batteries had been given for recharging at the workshop but unfortunately most of them had been damaged during enemy shelling.

The only alternative left was to handle-start. However, that was not an easy process. Two men had to stand on the handle and three men then needed to pull the rope tied to the handle with a jerk. Only after multiple attempts would the MACK truck start. This was not a practical approach as time was of the essence.

Mohinder Singh rose to the occasion and got hold of a few batteries. He started one MACK and hooked up one gun. He then removed the battery and used it to start the other MACKs, one by one and while hooking, every gun was loaded and primed ready to fire even on the move.

All this goes to show how one great Singh's initiative and intelligence saved the situation in the face of great odds and under relentless shelling and tank fire from the enemy.

L/Hav Mohinder Singh Dardi got mentioned in dispatches for his actions.

The IAF came in and continuous strafing and bombing halted the enemy's offensive short of Akhnoor. Only a counter offensive launched in Lahore eased the pressure against Chhamb.

□

12

The Incident

In mid 1972, 39 Medium settled in the 25 Infantry Division sector with Gun Batteries well deployed as follows :

- 122 Medium Battery was in troop strength at Krishna Ghati and Bimber Gali.
- 123 Medium Battery was at Dhral along with Regimental HQ at Talay Camp.
- 393 Medium Battery was in troop strength and deployed at Chetya Kabra/Kongata area.

Next to the gun area of one troop of 122 Medium Battery, 196 Mountain Regiment was deployed and there existed a small rivalry between the Khalsas of the two regiments based on the strength of muscle and fire power.

On 1st October, 1972, the OP officer at the frontline, deployed with 8 Sikh Regiment in 120 Infantry Brigade sector in Rajouri, noticed a major intrusion by Pakistani forces and thought it prudent to engage them with medium guns.

At that very same time, 196 Mountain Regimental Command Post was being manned by their doctor as the Unit Adjutant who had just taken a break had stepped back to the administrative area.

Alert levels were still very high and suddenly the frontline OP ordered medium fire. This was all new and too sudden for the doctor but he was able to relay the fire order to GPO.

Immediately the enemy had a couple of rounds of mediums landing on them and forcing them to retreat.

The OP in front, now satisfied with enemy retreat, ordered STOP to firing. The doctor, who was not well versed with stop-fire order, went outside the command post and casually shouted, "*Bas, bas*," to the GPO. The Gun Position Officer (GPO) acknowledged, "Das, das," and fired 10 more rounds. The doctor now had to physically run to the GPO to restrain the Khalsas from further firing. In the meantime 122 Medium battery had discarged over 20 rounds on the enemy.

It was not just the enemy that tasted the sheer fire power of the mediums of 122, but the 196 Khalsas felt it too. The window panes of 196 Mountain Regiment barracks were blown off and their sow gave premature birth. Unfortunately, all the piglets died, in turn settling the firepower rivalry between the two units.

Shanta Ram

123 Medium Battery was deployed at Dhral. The Battery OP was deployed at Shanta Ram, a captured post from the December 1971 operations. It was previously called Sukhanaban by the Pakistanis.

The Shanta Ram Post was barely 300 metres opposite the enemy and exchange of words was a regular feature.

The company deployed at this post was that of 4/1 Gorkha and Captain AK Kher was the Artillery OP.

Captain Kher's most trusted men – Santokh Singh and Ujjagar Singh were his radio operators and Gurmit Singh was the technical assistant.

The Company Commander at Shanta Ram was Major Chadha, who was an adventurous officer and got along very well with Captain Kher. Both the officers were hell bent on dominating the enemy opposite them and over many a drink, plans were hatched for ways to make life miserable for the enemy.

And the first occasion presented itself when one day an enemy goat crossed the LoC and came near Shanta Ram Post. The enemy had to be sent a message and the goat had to be made an example. The MMG-manning Jawan was ordered to fire one belt of ammunition on the goat. The goat was airborne for a minute at least.

Captain Kher then shouted across to the Pakistanis, "*Bakri ka haal dekha? Tum hamare area mein aayaa toh yeh hi haal hoga.*" Captain Kher had the biggest lungs and the voice to carry the message across clearly.

To further keep the enemy on the edge, it was decided that during PT time in the morning, except the men manning the weapons, the rest of the company would do the Khukri dance, which is ferocious and scary. It causes a chilling effect on an observer, who in this case being the enemy, was constantly watching us from 300 m away.

After midnight, a patrol would be sent to the line of control with kerosene-soaked garnish and tripwires. The patrol would then set fire to the enemy crop and come back. This caused panic in the enemy post and they would shout, "Oyee aa gaya Gorkha, jaldi stand toh karo." And the enemy would man their weapons and wait for the attack, staying alert all night. Now Shanta Ram post would relax and sleep peacefully, leaving the enemy awake the entire night.

And whenever this plan was executed, which was every other week, the 4/1 Gorkha sentry usually by 0200/0300 hours would report that a jeep light was seen approaching the enemy defences from their rear. Usually the enemy officers did not live with their troops. They lived in comfort, far behind their front lines. Due to the commotion caused by 4/1 Gorkha, the enemy would always psychologically be in fear and their officers on the edge.

During Captain Kher's stay with 4/1 Gorkha, he helped them to improve their defences. He noticed that their bunkers would not withstand medium fire.

On Diwali day, Captain Kher asked his 123 Medium Battery SJCO to invite Major Chadha's boys to gun area for a meal. 123 Medium Battery even provided two three - ton trucks for transporting them to the *badaa Khaana. (regimental party)* A good part of the 4/1 Gorkha Company came.

After the *badaa Khaana*, a demonstration of medium-gun drill was presented. On Captain Kher's instructions, the Gorkhas were asked to lift a medium shell. It took four Gorkhas to pick up one shell which was usually handled by a single Khalsa.

The end result was that on the return to Post Shanta Ram, every 4/1 Gorkha Jawan was repairing and strengthening his bunkers and shelters to withstand the eventuality of a medium shell landing on them.

Dominating the enemy in eyeball-to-eyeball deployment was complete.

39 Medium Regiment remained deployed in 25 Infantry Division area, facing the Pakistanis until 1973, after which it was ordered to move to 33 Corps sector under the Eastern Command and deploy in Sikkim to face the Chinese.

Captain Kher's 123 Medium Battery had smooth handing/ taking over and the Battery signed no deficiencies, thanks to MT Hav Mukthar Singh and his EME friend at the workshop.

Of the other two Medium Batteries, the CO and Commander of the Artillery Brigade had to literally beg the OC workshop to help and despite that, they paid and signed deficiencies. It took them two years to sort out the deficiencies.

□

13

Capt AK Kher

Kher's unit 127 Division Locating Battery moved from Amritsar to Jaurian in December 1970 and was stationed alongside the 18 Field Regiment.

During the early summer of 1971, Captain Kher took part in operation alerts of 191 Infantry Brigade where roles and conduct of battle in defence of Chhamb by PAPA and QUEBEC forces were thoroughly practiced on ground with the armoured regiment.

During May/June 1971, Brigadier Henry Srinivasan, Commander of 10 Artillery Brigade visited 127 Division Locating Battery and took along Captain Kher for reconnaissance in 191 Infantry Brigade sector. Brigadier Srinivasan generally tasked Captain Kher to establish a theater grid in 10 Infantry Division sector and link it up with 26 Infantry Division deployed in east Jammu, Samba region, and 25 Infantry Division in the north, deployed to defend Poonch to Naushera. After this task was given by the Commander, Captain Kher was dispatched on annual leave and on return was ordered to commence this task.

Upon returning from his annual leave, Captain Kher commenced the task. This involved occupying and taking observations from every high ground in the 10 Infantry Division sector to obtain knowledge of every track, every village and every high ground in the entire Division area. He was slowly able to link up 26 Infantry Division at Akhnoor Fort by having a common Bearing Post (BP) and in 25 Infantry Division he linked up with Kalidhar GOC 1 and GOC 2 Posts.

All future gun areas and main gun areas' BPs were established. All the guns were linked up with OPs on the grid. Captain Kher further took the initiative and fixed control points in enemy territory for deployment in case of 10 Infantry Division's advance into Pakistan.

He also flew multiple air observation missions with Captain Padmanabhan (Paddy) before and during the hot war. In FDC, during the war, he manned the 'fire order' line, maintaining battle logs and situation maps.

Captain AK Kher was also in constant communication with all the units throughout the duration of the war. On a number of occasions, on the 3rd, 4th and 5th December, 1971, he visited ALG, 12 Field Regiment, 81 Field Regiment, 216 and

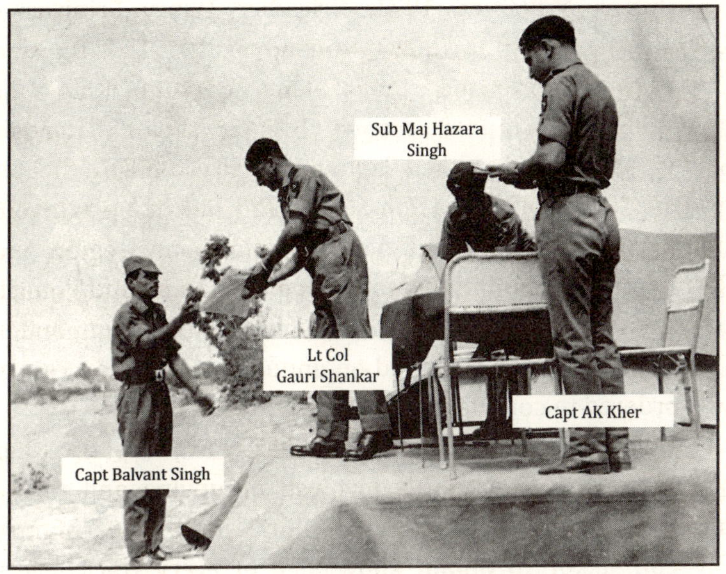

39 Medium Regiments with fire plans and reported first hand ground information to Brigade Commander, Henry Srinivasan.

Prior to the breaking out of hostilities, he was posted to 39 Medium Regiment, but since there was no replacement at Artillary Brigade HQ, he was not relieved by the Brigade Commander to join the Regiment. The 39 Medium Regiment had shifted its Mess to a new dugout and as Captain Kher was visiting the Regiment on routine, he was made the guest of honour in the new Mess with CO Lt Col Gauri Shankar announcing his dining in.

Captain AK Kher left FDC after the ceasefire. He saluted Brigadier Srinivasan and told him that he was joining 39 Medium. While a CO conference was on, the Brigadier got up, hugged Kher and thanked him for all he had done during the war.

Brigadier Srinivasan wrote on Captain Kher's war ACR: "Ashok Kher is a brave officer." He even graced Captain Kher's wedding reception at India International Centre in New Delhi in September 1974.

Captain AK Kher joined the 39 Medium Regiment as Battery Captain (BK) 123 Medium Battery at Pahari Wala gun area, a day after the ceasefire was declared. His Battery Commander (BC) was Major HS Dhinsa, who was a soldiers' soldier and had a considerable influence on Captain Kher's personality. Major Dhinsa and his wife, who was a professor at Punjab University, even graced Captain Kher's ancestral village-home in Kashmir and stayed a day at his house.

Captain Kher served 39 Medium Regiment till 1974 and was posted out thereafter joined the Regiment back as Major in 1982 at Basoli Camp, Jammu and stayed on for a further seven-year stint with the unit.

Wedding Reception at India International Centre

A few years later, in 1985, he had the privilege of commanding the 1st Battery of 130 mm Guns on Siachen Glaciers in the 102 Infantry Brigade sector.

From 1986 to July 1988, he was 2IC of 39 Medium and the unit took part in Operation Brasstacks, the largest military exercise conducted by India in the Thar Desert.

Finally Lt Col AK Kher had the honour of commanding 39 Medium Regiment from 25th July, 1988 to 18th March, 1989. During the tenure of Lt Col AK Kher, 39 Medium was a champion in almost all the events held in 18 Infantry Division at Alwar, Rajasthan.

CO Lt Col Ashok Kher addressing 39 Medium Regiment

The narration of the battle of Chhamb in 1971 is a factual account of what he witnessed and recorded. Being based at the prime control-and-communication centre of Artillery Fire Direction Centre, he had a clear understanding of the events as they unfolded. All the officers named on the front line were either personally known to Captain Kher or met by him while carrying out survey work for 10 Artillery Brigade over the course of one-and-a-half years.

□

VOLUME II

MOVE TO CHINA BORDER

14

Train to the East

39 Medium Regiment moved from Nowshera to Pathankot by road and then to Siliguri by train (Rolling Stock) Military Special.

During those days, in 1973, the food in the *langar* was cooked on coal and firewood. Supplies of coal and firewood would always fall short as the scales authorised by the Ministry of Defence (MOD) in Delhi were invariably inadequate.

The Military Special halted at Asansol station. On the adjacent line, a long goods train with open racks full of coal, was stationed. A hush-hush voice sounded on the Military Special, "*Koyla, oye koyla*" and in minutes one rake of 20 tons got empty!

The coal-train driver noticed this pilferage and complained to CO Lt Col Rathore. The CO along with the complaining driver searched the entire Military Special train. A meagre 10 kgs of coal was found and this was promptly and apologetically returned.

All officers of 39 Medium were dumbfounded – *aakhir koyla kidhar gaya?* (Where did the coal vanish?) Ajit Singh Padree, our *langar* commander, told Captain Kher, "*Asi koyla kote chi, hathyaran thala choopaya, utha kay na dakhna see.*" (We hid the coal in the armoury under the arms and nobody could have looked for it there).

Ajit Singh was known as Padree in the unit and nobody actually knew his real name. At Meerut Cantonment, much before the 1971 war, behind the regimental area, there was an old church. Ajit Singh was its caretaker and he maintained it as good as the *Gurdwara Sahib*. Every day, he lit candles at the altar and on Sundays he would distribute *prasad*. For his actions he was called 'Padree', a name that stuck with him till he retired from military service.

Upon reaching Siliguri, the angry CO Lt Col Rathore ordered a display of the entire equipment.

A motorcycle, one jeep trailer, 36 new gun tyres and 40 Kraz tyres were found to be in surplus. These tyres came in very handy during inspections, especially Kraz tyres, as there was always a shortage of them.

The Kraz gun tower was of Russian origin and its spares, like headlights, sidelights and doorknobs were not available in the local market and had to be imported along with tyres. These were essentials, as without them, vehicles presented a shabby look during the inspections. However, 39 Medium never failed an ADM inspection and their vehicles were always *tanatan* (shining).

A *khufya janch partal* (undercover unofficial investigation) revealed that the unit had a sizeable reserve of these items hidden in the MT (mechanical transport) stores.

A deeper probe revealed that during the 1971 operations, while withdrawing under heavy Pakistani bombardment on 6th December, 1971 night, 39 Medium Khalsas created the surplus spares. In their farsighted approach and unmindful of life and limb, they picked up whatever came in sight in the neighbourhood.

Unfortunately the CO ordered destruction of the motorcycle, jeep trailer, Kraz and gun tyres which was done with tearful eyes.

□

15

Welcome to Sikkim

The Indian Army's Eastern Command is based at Fort William in Calcutta and was commanded by Lt General NC Rawlley, back in 1973.

The Trishakti Corps/XXXIII Corps came under the Eastern Command. Head quartered at Siliguri, it was dedicated to guarding the sensitive McMahon Line with China.

33 Corps Area

The elements of 33 Corps comprised of: 17 Mountain Division commanded by Major General Kalyer guarding Nathu La and Sikkim with HQ at Gangtok.

27 Mountain Division commanded by Major General Dalbir Singh guarding Jelep La and Bhutan with HQ at Kalimpong.

20 Mountain Division based in Binnaguri for its role in Bhutan, commanded by Major General Lachhman Singh Lehl PVSM, VrC, who was ex-39 Medium.

33 Corps had an Artillery Brigade and Commander (CC) Artillery was Brigadier Mahal.

Route Map from Siliguri to Gangtok

39 Medium Regiment was on the move from Siliguri in a convoy to Mile 7. The Gangtok Nathu La Road was narrow and mountainous. Strictly only one-way traffic was allowed and this area was controlled by Corps of Military Police (CMP).

Some fancy car came up behind the convoy and kept on constantly honking and trying to overtake. They had managed to overtake some vehicles but due to limitation in the width of the road, got stuck in between the convoy.

When the convoy halted, the Sikkim locals came out of the car and started bellowing expletives at the Sardars and even calling them 'Bloody Indians'. The Singhs didn't take this kindly and with their heads inside, through the windows of the car, told the nice looking Sikkim ladies, "*Oye* bloody Indians, *hoy hoy*!" and they then proceeded to physically lift the car with bare hands and put it to the side of the road in sheer display of Khalsa strength.

On reaching Mile 7, CO Lt Col Rathore was immediately hauled up into the GOC's office and given a tongue-lashing. The folks in the fancy car were Sikkim's royal family members. Sikkim was ruled by the Chogyal, who was the absolute monarch until then.

39 Medium Regiment was deployed and comprised of the following:

122 Medium Battery, commanded by Major JRK Bhattacharji, along with the Regimental HQ, was deployed in Menla at ridge area, near 17 Milestone, in support of 17 Mountain Division.

123 Medium Battery was deployed in support of 27 Mountain Division at Wood Cock, defending Jelep La Pass. This pass lies at an elevation of 14,390 feet in the Dongkya Range of the eastern Himalayas. The Battery was commanded by Major Bharat Singh with Captain Kher officiating mostly.

In 1973, Woodcock was the highest Medium gun position in the world. The guns were of 5.5 inch calibre with a range of 18,100 yds and with each shell weighing 80 lbs. 393 Medium Battery commanded by Major Dhinsa was stationed at Siliguri itself.

39 Medium Regiment was not new to the area. Under Operation Liston, they were deployed in Sikkim on 23rd October, 1962 for the protection of Nathu La Pass against Chinese aggression. At that time, only a dirt track existed up to Gangtok and then a narrow track with a ropeway led up to Nathu La.

The regiment HQ was to be positioned at Goyearkata with Major Didar Singh leading 122 Medium Battery, which was divided in troop strength among Changu Lake area, Rangpo and Milestone 4 on Gangtok's Nathu La Road. The guns had to be deployed in higher areas, which were in extremely treacherous terrain.

In 1962, 5.5 inch guns being assembled at Changu Lake area

Each of the gun detachments was manned by 10 *Khunkhar* (dangerous) Singhs. The gun was towed by a MACK (six-wheeled heavy truck). Even to drive on such roads, one needed balls of steel. On one such drive for deployment up the high mountains, the road under the MACK caved in, overlooking a steep fall of 600 feet. The brave driver, a Singh, pulled off a miracle and drove over the mountainside incline. The entire detachment sung praises of that driver, "*Singh nay kamal kita, gaddi aur gun ek side pahad tay chadaye*" and saved the gun detachment from falling over.

The GOC came in person to see this feat of Khalsaji and congratulated the driver, asking him, "*Kya mangta hai Singh*?" (What do you want?). Singh, after a good thought, said, "*Sahib ik botal XXX de do.*" (Sir, one bottle of XXX rum.)

Assembled Gun at Changu Lake area in 1962

After the GOC left, the detachment pounced on him, "*Oye ullu, havaldari mangta, taraqqi mangta General Sahib tanu kuch bhi de sakde see.*" (Idiot, you could have asked to be promoted to Havaldar. General could give you anything out of turn).

Singh said, "*Mannu kuch samaj nahi aya, Hafta hoya peete naye, manu botal hi deekhe.*" (I could only think of alcohol as I have not had a drink for a week.)

Deployment continued at Changu to defend Nathu La Pass in Sikkim. However beyond Gangtok, only a dirt track existed and it was impossible to move guns on the terrain which did not permit MACK truck movement.

Not to be bogged down by the difficulty ahead, L/Nk Shiv Singh, the gun-fitter of 122 Medium Battery, came up with an ingenious solution. He dismantled the big guns and loaded their parts in one-ton vehicles so that the movement to Changu area could be possible. This was a critical time as guns were to be in place before the ceasefire came into effect with China and to provide cover fire in case of further aggression.

For his heroics of dismantling/assembling guns and bringing them into action in record time, the regimental gun-fitter L/Nk Shiv Singh earned the Chief's commendation card way back in 1962.

□

16

Mundane Life at 14,000 Feet above Mean Sea Level

Jelep La Pass

Bille Patrol

Once every month, Captain Kher used to go on a patrol where he and the patrol party would walk around a kilometre in front of the Chinese defences at Jelep La. The Chinese would always get on 'Stand To' the moment they saw the Indian patrol approaching, meaning they would get into firing positions, fix bayonets, arm grenades and be ready to attack or defend.

If the Indian patrol included 20 Jawans, 24 Chinese armed men would walk alongside, shoulder to shoulder, with this patrol in front of their defences. At that time, the Chinese would wear cheap-material uniforms, but generally clean.

On one such occasion, Padree Ajit Singh was with Captain Kher as wireless operator.

Padree remarked to Captain Kher, "*Sahib, Chini pachan gya tusi afsar ho.*".(The Chinese have recognised that you as our officer.)

Captain Kher, "*Kedda*?. (How?)

Padree, "*Ma dekhya peecha ina da political commissar toda wall chadi dekha raya see.*" (I saw the political commissar at the back was pointing his stick at you.)

Padree, giving *taav* (twirling) his moustache towards the Chinese, "*Sahib ik gal puccha*?" (Can I ask a question?)

Captain Kher, "*Jes.*" (Yes)

Captain AK Kher at Woodcock Gun Area

Padree, now winking at the Chini and walking closer to him, said, "*Sahib yeah badya chikne ha, mada ja order deyo toh ik fad ka laa chalan langar tay kam angey*."(They look really nice, just give the order and I will kidnap one and take with me for he will be well utilised in the kitchen.)

This is the true state of mind of a good Khalsa warrior in front of the enemy bayonets.

The Chinese Singh, L/Nk Lakha

We had our own Chinese-looking Singh, who had Mongoloid features with high cheekbones and 10 or 15 hairs on his chin and about 6 or 7 hairs on the upper lip on either side, in lieu of a moustache. He had passed the intermediate exam and was a *padalekha* (educated) Sardar. His father was a Sikh who had married a Chinese woman, while working in Burma.

Lakha Singh was well liked and would always entertain the unit on *badaa khaana* (regimental party) with Chinese-sounding songs, which used to be a big hit with the men. The lyrics would always be something like "*Meya feyad ga ching ching hoy oye...*" At Woodcock Gun Position, while on night duty, Lakha Singh was caught sleeping at his post which is unacceptable for a Sikh soldier. Now, if he were to be marched up, he would lose his rank. Captain Kher did not wish that Lakha should lose his rank, so Lakha was given a choice to decide on his punishment – official or unofficial, it was for him to choose. He wisely chose unofficial and was awarded 30 extra duties (not by any military manual). Lakha Singh stood on duty for 20 days and on the 21st day he dropped to the ground exhausted. Mind you, this was at a high altitude with snow of about 8 or 10 feet. Lakha was produced in front of Captain Kher for further action. A Battery fall in was announced with

Lakha standing in front of the Battery.

But instead, Captain AK Kher acclaimed Lakha as a great Sikh warrior who had stood his post for 20 days without a complaint in extremely tough conditions, showing determination and devotion to duty.

L/Nk Lakha Singh, not only held his rank and pay, but was also sent on 30 days' extra leave (unauthorised) and was awarded 20 bottles of rum as a token of appreciation for the grit he displayed.

Gunner Roop Singh Balde

For the annual inspection of Woodcock gun position CC Artillery Brigadier Mahal was to inspect the Battery. Roop Singh was a gunner at the gun-post which was convenient for any VIP to visit due to its location.

Captain Kher knew Roop would be the Commander's target and would be grilled about gunnery. He made sure that every effort was made to thoroughly prepare and rehearse Roop Singh so as to sail through the visit. As expected, the Commander came to Roop's gun position and put the obvious questions to him. Gunner Roop Singh replied, "*Sahibji, apan tay loader han, aa saval No 1 ustad ko puccho.*"

(I am just a loader; please ask your questions from Gun No. 1.)

All officers in the Battery were left baffled with Roop's volte face. After the departure of Commander; GPO (Gun Position Officer) Lieutenant Tandon came to Captain Kher and explained the situation, which turned out to be the greatest joke of the day. Gunner Roop Singh in ceremonial dress, during the inspection was wearing snowboots and both of which were for left foot. "How the hell could that happen?" exclaimed Captain Kher.

Lieutenant Tandon replied, "Well, the Commander's chopper was late and the men had been standing for long.

They were ordered to break off on hearing about the delay."

The Men took off their boots and relaxed in their lines; however, shortly someone shouted, "*Aaa guyaa oye.*" (He has arrived). They put on their boots in a hurry and ran. Gunner Roop Singh was last to leave the barrack and found that his right boot had been misplaced; he remained with two left ones. He tried his best to find the right shoe; even a search in the stock dump turned out to be futile. So Roop's only option to prevent the Commander from noticing this major flaw was by deflecting the question itself.

Roop Singh's answer to GPO for his misdemeanour towards the Commander was by giving a twist to his scraggy moustache and saying, "*Commander nay to nahye fadya.*" (At least the Commander didn't catch me.)

This was not the only time when Roop Singh displayed his funny interpretation.

In 1965, when Roop Singh was Captain Mahmood's orderly. Captain Mahmood said to Roop Singh, "Roop Singh, *Mess may ja akhbar la, khabar-shaber padhya.*"

After one hour, Roop Singh returned with a *kassi* (digging instrument).

"*Sahib Mess ma koye nahi mila; dasoo kabbar kethey khodney hai*?" (I didn't find anyone in the Mess; tell me where to dig the grave?)

Officers' Mess Staff

In the Officers' Mess, waiters and cooks were a great team and always took good care of the officers. Masalchi Doonichand usually officiated as Mess Havaldar and was outstanding at his work.

Doonichand, be it in desert, mountain or anywhere, for a big party could produce material for the choicest menu from nowhere; his only requirement was a vehicle and one bottle of XXX. Every month he had to be bailed out from the local police station as he was a ladies' man and invariably got caught!

Tau Sohan Lal, the elderly Haryanavi waiter, was caring and faithful. He would serve drinks at the bar and keep the young officers under watch. He served within limits and in case officers tended to exceed, he would say, "*Sahib bus karo. CO Sahib dekh raha hai. Kal long-range patrol per bhejega*" (LRP). (CO is watching and tomorrow he will send you on long- range patrol).

That would mean the end of happiness for 10 days.

Joginder was the Mess attendant and during a conversation, he would always add *ji* to everything. A telephone call comes to the Mess. Joginder picks up the receiver.

Captain Kher: "*Joginder, lunch da menu kya hai*? (What is the lunch menu?)

Joginder: *Sabziji, dalji, saladji, murga sham vastay ji* (chicken is for evening), fruit *nahi aya ji, Kela ha ji* (fruit didn't come today; only banana)! *Sat sri Akalji*."

Once Joginder went on annual leave. After 60 days, on his return, he looked pale and thin with all the flab gone and barely recognisable.

Captain Kher: "*Oye Joginderji aa kya hoya*? (What happened?)

Tau, the elderly attendant, replied, "*Sahib, pind kam karonday Joginder nu* (in the village, they make him work) *pandraa din ma theek ho jaye* (in 15 days, he'll be okay.)Captain Kher: *Kayda*? (How?)

Tau: *Ayena langar tay daily char char dolu daal pee laynay dus/pandraa dina chi pher daddu ban jaou*. (He will drink 4/4 mugs of *daal* and become a fat frog again in 10/15 days.)

Gunner Dalbir Singh, the Gorilla

Dalbir was the Battery store-man, in charge of rations. He was a highly *jugaadu* man and well known as 'Gorilla' for his monkey-like antics. Usually special items of officers' rations, like ham, bacon, sausages, cheese, etc. as per the authorised scale were not enough for a single officer in the Battery. It would take two months for issue of a tin of sausages from supply store and poor Dalbir would get an earfull every day for it.

Captain Kher, "*Officers', ration kiddar hai? Ainvayi hi 'Gorilla' banta.*" (Where is the officers' ration and you pretend to be a gorilla?)

Gorilla approached OC supplies, requesting for couple of tins of officers' rations. The OC did a calculation and told him, "*Tera kucch be naye banta aglay saal aana.*" (There is nothing pending for you; come next year.)

Gorilla pleaded, "*Meri izzat rakhlo saab,*" but the OC refused to oblige.

Not to be dissuaded, next day the Gorilla went to the Supplies, ordered his driver to keep the vehicle on the main road facing the direction of Woodcock with the engine running, door open and ordered the driver to remain in the seat. He then went to the Army Supply Corps (ASC) store, informed the store-in-charge that the OC has called him urgently.

The moment the Havaldar left to see his OC, Gorilla barged into the store and quickly filled his bag with officers' ration tins and ran to his vehicle. There was a big *hulla-gulla* (commotion) in the depo but Gorilla was well past their area.

The OC Supply rang up Captain Kher and informed him about the grave indiscipline of our man, but adding., "I admire the man for his motivation. He did ask me for help but due to rules I couldn't oblige. Please do not initiate any action."

Thus the 'gorilla' lived up to his name.

Tiger Joginder Singh

A well-built handsome Khalsa was our Regimental Police (RP) man at Woodcock gun position and was known as Tiger. Usually officers wore parkas without rank badges and many would not draw a salute. So to ensure every officer was saluted who passed the Battery gate, he would throw a smart salute to every vehicle passing through.

Tiger was also in-charge of a live goat kept for slaughter for the unit's Raising Day celebration. Unfortunately one day the goat went missing and a massive search yielded no result. Tiger lost face; men started poking fun at him. He lost his title TIGER. Men would now instead call him Tango Joginder.

Joginder was hurt and restless as he took pride in his title of 'Tiger'. He took it upon himself to restore his honour and finally his efforts in *jasoosi* (investigation) paid result.

The neighbouring unit's JCOs had stolen and eaten the goat. He met their SM (Subedar Major) and asked for a goat in lieu; however, the SM shooed him away. Tango then went to the gun position where the CO lived and put up his case. The CO asked for proof, but Tango had no witnesses or evidence to show and had to retreat.

Like a true tiger stalking his prey, Joginder found the remains of the goat buried in the JCO's Mess. He dug the remains out, took them to the CO. Now with this irrefutable evidence in hand, Tango, instead of one, demanded two goats as compensation. He sat down outside the CO's bunker and refused to yield any ground till his demand was met.

Captain Kher was not aware of these happenings and was surprised to get a call from the CO. The CO apologised for the conduct of his JCOs and requested Kher to tell Tango to come back to the Battery and promised to make good his loss.

Next day, the SM of the neighbouring unit came to 123 Med Battery and handed over two goats to Tango.

Tango's title now stood restored to Tiger with honour. Later, in a few years' time, Tiger's younger brother cleared the Services Selection Board and became an officer in the Indian Army.

Trilochan Singh and MT Hav Mukthar Singh

Trilochan was a big *zamindar* and a matriculation pass. He would speak only English after downing a few drinks and repeat, "My MT (Military Transport) fit for, no off road." Normally he would get hold of the CO and repeat the same and no one would mind.

In sub-zero temperature and in heavy snow, vehicular batteries would freeze. At best, the vehicle would crank once and go dead as the cold engine would not start. Mukthar Singh had found an ingenious way of starting vehicles.

One day Captain Kher saw a fire was lit in the MT which is forbidden in the Army for obvious reasons. On close inspection, he found a mesh of the air cleaner deliberately set on fire.

Captain Kher bellowed, "*Mukthar aa ki ho raha ha*?" (What is this happening?)

Mukthar, "*Sahibji air cleaner guram kar rahan hoon; guram air cleaner engine tay rakh ka self mare da upparun gharam hava lung kay ondi hay gaddi, ik self che start hondi hay.*" (I am heating up the air cleaner so that the heated air goes into the engine and it starts with one self.) Totally against regulations, but no choice!

Accident of Khalsaji

Sikkim's mountainous terrain left two Jawans badly injured with two vehicles written off in an accident.

Khalsaji's statement in the court of enquiry (COI) was,

"Sahibji, I was deputed to go down to fetch stores from the maintenance company and I told my no. 1 to depute someone else for this job. I specifically informed him, Majorji *mere khabi ankh fudak rahe hay manu kuch changa naye lag raha hay*." (My left eye is blinking and I don't feel right; kindly send somebody else.)

Instead of listening to me, he did not change my duty. I checked oil, water, lights, brakes of my vehicle, topped the petrol tank, filled the duty-on-car diary and also got it signed. I followed all the correct procedures.

I started my vehicle and while leaving the gate, "*Manu gurudwara da nishan sahib dekhya, ma hath joday wahay garu aaj menu baccha na*." (I saw Gurudwara Nishan Sahib and even washed my hands and bowed to Guru and requested for protection.)

While going down, there was fog. "*Dour saay manu Gorkhaja dikhya. Gaddi lay kay upper aa raha see, ma kahaya 'Wahe Guru baccha,, aye mera accident karu ga, ma gaddi reverse che pa deye.' Aaj bhi tusi ja ka dekho meri gaddi reverse gear che khaddi hai*." (From far I saw a Gorkha-looking guy driving his vehicle up and I immediately prayed to Wahe Guru that this guy will cause an accident, please save me and I put my vehicle in reverse gear to save myself and you can even check my vehicle is still in reverse gear.)

The presiding officer took him to the site and what they saw was the Gorkha's vehicle correctly on his side of the road and Khalsaji's vehicle almost on top of the bonnet of Gorkha's vehicle.

The presiding officer asked, "*Singhji, ay kedan hoya*?" (How do you explain this?)

"*Sahibji, ayhe tay pata nahi, kiddan hoya*." (This exactly is what I myself am perplexed about and don't know how it happened.)

Cheetah Observation Post

An Artillery Observation Post had been established on the adjoining high feature which overlooked the Yatung area for several kilometres and the Yatung Gompha could be seen from here. This Observation Post provided a magnificent view of all the areas deep into Chumbi Valley.

The height of the post was approximately 16,500 feet above sea level and the most difficult part was the last 200 feet climb to reach the top. It was exactly at 90 degrees incline and had to be scaled by using ropes.

This was a unique post. Usually there would be clear sunshine as it was above the cloud level but in the rainy season, the place acted like a magnet for lightning strikes. Just before a strike, a peculiar sound 'zeee zeee' could be heard, which acted like a warning for all to jump on to a wooden plank inside the bunker and wrap themselves in a blanket. And on cue, the lightning would strike, followed by a deafening thunder!

This post had three levels – the top-level bunker was manned by an Artillery OP officer, the second level was an OP party bunker and the lower level had a bunker for a section of Infantry. There was no operating toilet here and in the limited space around the post itself, one had no choice but to go out.

The Artillery OP party usually occupied the Post for a period of 10 days and then was replaced by others. This time Captain AK Kher with radio operator Santok Singh (later RHM and JA at Alwar), Gurdav Singh and two more Jawans were on top. This was the most desolated Post covered with human faeces all over!! A sweeper, Rambhajan, had to be brought up for a day to clean up the top-level bunker and rest of the Post area.

Psycological Warfare Khalsa Style

The Chinese had installed loudspeakers at Nathu La and these on a regular basis would warn the Indian side to withdraw. The Khalsas of Sikh LI deployed there had designed a unique response to such a call.

The Sardarjis on sentry duty at the Post facing the Chinese, whenever the need arose to pee would step out of the post. They would face the Chinese, open the buttons of the woollen trousers, put their hand inside their long Johns, whip out their personal weapon and let it spray towards the Chinese.

The Chinese soldiers, facing them, would always be offended and shout obscenities, spitting on the ground and stamping it. Maybe it meant something in Chinese culture but our Khalsas, in reply, would only brush up their moustache, shake and holster the personal weapon inside. The Khalsas' psychological warfare forced the Chinese to give duty inside their bunkers.

Raid on Banniya of 199 Mountain Regiment

199 Mountain Regiment was about one kilometre on a lower plateau than the 123 Medium gun positions at Woodcock. Sometimes men would go down to buy provisions from the Banniya of 199 Mountain Regiment.

Captain AK Kher had to go to Varanasi for PABT (Pilot Aptitude and Battery Test) to qualify for Air OP training. Lieutenant Dutta was sent from Siliguri to officiate in place of Captain Kher.

One day, Lieutenant Dutta and Gunner Hamir Singh went below to the wet canteen (Banniya) of 199 Mountain Regiment. Lieutenant Dutta asked him about some item and the Banniya was extremely rude. Despite Lieutenant Dutta identifying himself as Gun Position Officer (GPO) of the Medium Battery, the Banniya continued speaking rudely to him.

Lieutenant Dutta reported this to 2 IC Major Jog of 199, who called the Banniya and asked him to apologise. However, instead of a sincere apology, the arrogant Banniya said, "*Theek hai Sahib, aap boltey han to maa mafi mangta hoon.*" (As you are insisting, I apologise).

This incident did not go down well with Gunner Hamir Singh. On return to the Battery, at dinner, he suddenly threw down his plate, started crying and narrated the incident in the *langar*. The men, on hearing Hamir Singh, took it as a serious personal insult to them. They, along with BHM Jagit Singh (GD) went down, ransacked the Banniya's shop and beat him and his staff up badly.

BHM Jagit Singh thundered, "*Apane sahib sa tum dilo mafhi mango* or we will come with our rifles and if we are not satisfied, we will turn our Mediums and blow you to bits." Not even a soul of 199 Regiment was seen to intervene with or placate the Khalsas.

Commanding Officer 199 Mountain Regiment made a case of arson, vandalism and loot against 123 Medium Battery and reported them to the local Station HQ. The investigating officers from HQ along with 199 Regiment Jawans came to 123 Battery at Woodcock for identification parade. After the parade broke off, the Battery, seething with anger, shouted the war cry of "*Jo bole so nihal, Sat Sri Akal*" and surrounded the entire Station HQ investigation party.

The situation turned extremely precarious and somehow the HQ officers, with great tact, managed to save themselves and leave gracefully with their dignity intact.

In the meantime Captain AK Kher returned from Varanasi. The CC Artillery Brigadier Mahal flew in from Siliguri and 39 CO Lt Col Rathore came from Menla to investigate the incident.

Captain Kher received a high dose of warning from both the Commander and CO and was told that he was held accountable for the kind of motivation that the men had exhibited.

Captain AK Kher had to give a written apology to CO Lt Col Bahel of 199 Mountain Regiment.

Ammunition Maintenance

At every other Gun Post of Artillery Brigade in Sikkim, the ammo was dumped in bunkers. The bunkers, being usually over the snow line, were affected by seepages which were very high and thus damaged the ammo.

The entire Artillery ammo of the formation was designated Repair Major Required (RMJ), except for 39 Medium Regiment's.

The ammo in every gun position of 39 Medium Regiment was a hundred percent fit and serviceable. Commander 27 Mountain Artillery Brigade was very impressed and ordered Captain Kher to organise a demonstration for the brigade on how to maintain ammo at high altitude.

The Khalsas of 39 Medium had developed a procedure through experience and followed it diligently to store ammo. The Khalsas had put boulders in the bunkers and over them placed tin sheets at a slight incline. This facilitated the water to quickly drain and they made sure the ammo was kept away from the bunker walls by 7/8 inches.

This common-sense approach saved the ammo and maintenance.

□

17

Extra Initiative of the Singhs

Jelep La Pass led to the Chumbi Valley of the Tibetan Plateau. Nathu La and Jelep La Pass were the ancient passages through the Himalayas and used for trade and cultural exchange between Tibet and Sikkim until 1962.

On the Indian side, there are two routes to Jelep La, one through Gangtok and the other via Kalimpong passing through Pedong in northern West Bengal, Rhenok and Kupup.

Jelep La Pass itself is held by Chinese troops. The Nathu La Pass and the heights overlooking the Jelep La Pass are held by Indian troops. Any Chinese ingress via Jelep La Pass is observed and controlled by the Lal Quila defensive complex located on the heights. This complex dominated the Chinese defences on the watershed by observation and fire.

On the right of the Lal Quila complex outside the Battalion defended area was the Cheetha OP. Much to the right of Cheetha OP was a big hill feature, which used to be occupied by 4 Sikh LI during operation alerts.

A Chinese-defended locality was on the opposite side of this hill feature and was at an odd inaccessible place from the Chinese side. It was vacated by the Chinese troops during the winter months which are practically all year round.

After a long period of time, upon the melting of snow, a Chinese patrol was observed in the area following which a diplomatic protest trickled in from New Delhi. According to protocol, the Chinese had called for a flag meeting and a very strong protest was lodged by them.

They alleged that their entire defences in the area opposite to Sikh LI were stripped of about 1,000 CGI tin sheets. An in-house enquiry was ordered by the higherups and that reluctantly revealed Khalsaji's standard answer, "*Sanu ki pata see yeh Chinaya de they. Ladger charge tay haga, sal bar ethay koye disa naye, asi spare samaj ka puut laye; ab wapas naye ho sakta, sheetan tay assi baksay banatay.*" (We didn't know the sheets belonged to the Chinese. We saw nobody using them for a year and though they are spare sheets that could be better

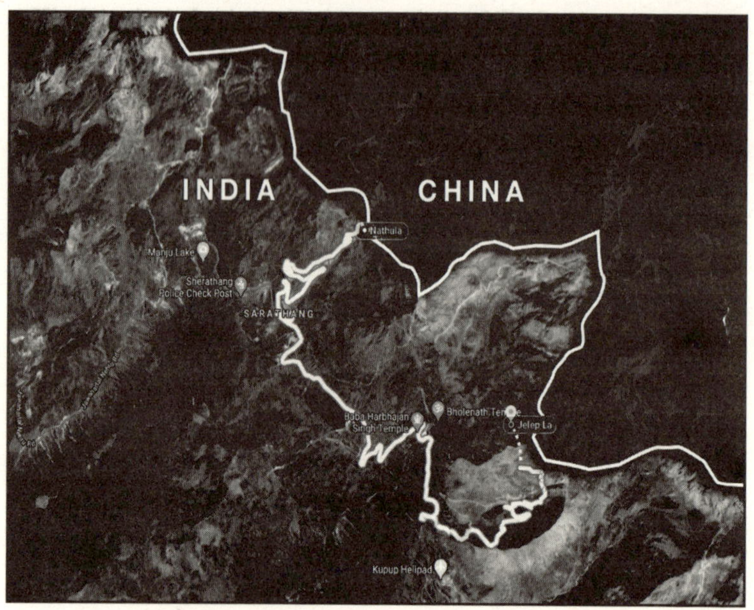

Feature Map of Nathu La and Jelep La (Google Maps)

utilised by us, but now we can't return these sheets as they've been converted into boxes.) After much discussion Sikh LI Singhs returned about 50/60 sheets.

Captain AK Kher also had a tin box which actually lasted for many postings.

□

18

Goodbye Sikkim, Welcome Darangdara

After a mundane life at Sikkim, in early 1974 Captain AK Kher in May had his posting orders to join 126 Division Locating Battery in Darangdara, Gujarat in the 11 Infantry Division sector.

11/Golden Katar Infantry Division, also known as the Desert Division, had its HQ in Ahmadabad and was commanded by Major General K Sundarji.

126 Division Locating Battery was commanded by Major Dewan. It was part of 11 Artillery Brigade commanded by Brigadier A Kaul.

After the usual dining in, Captain Kher settled in as 2IC.

Uniforms are switched to khaki here to blend in with the terrain.

A Messy Incident

The radar section of the Locating Battery needed a shed as it stood exposed to rain and shine. Aditionally the unit Quarter Guard with Armoury lacked a fence, causing security issues. Captain Kher put in a few requisitions to set up a shed and a fence for the protection of national assets but unfortunately no response was forthcoming from either the Brigade HQ or Military Engineering Service (MES).

Not far from 126 Division Locating Battery, an MES yard was located. This yard was full of angle irons and was well guarded day and night.

After waiting for a year for the shed and fence to be set up and noting that nothing was being done by MES or Brigade HQ, it was decided by Captain Kher to take matters in his own hands in the interest of protecting India's national assets. He directed his men to get some angle irons from the MES yard for using them for the unit's essential shed-and-fence needs.

The radar shed requirement was met, the fencing of Quarter Guard done and out of the remaining iron, stands of basketball posts were made.

The men did not urgently paint the angle irons due to lethargy and left the pickets as they were.

Unfortunately one picket of the Quarter Guard fence had the marking 'DHD MES' which was visible as the Quarter Guard faced the road. On passing by, the MES personnel noticed this and they promptly did a stocktaking of their yard and found 28 tons of angle iron missing.

126 Division Locating Battery was caught and Captain Kher rightly held responsible for this flub. Captain Kher incorrectly assumed that these men were like 39 Medium, his previous unit boys who were experts in managing these things.

Brigadier A Kaul was on leave and Col LAP Sequeira CO of 41 Field Regiment was officiating as Station Commander. He directed a formal investigation against Captain AK Kher, who was caught in a real thick soup. Enquiry commenced and some bigwigs came from Division HQ, Ahmedabad to carry out the investigations.

Meanwhile, Commander Brigadier Kaul came back from leave and when the issue was reported to him, he asked the presiding officer about the enquiry and what exactly Captain Kher had done with the angle irons. Brigadier Kaul was then given the details about the shed, fence and basketball stand.

Upon understanding the situation, Commander Kaul told the presiding officer of the enquiry that Captain Kher had demonstrated only good intentions to protect his unit's precious equipment and so long as he did not take anything home or sell it in the open market, he did not deserve to be hanged for this.

Brigadier Kaul ordered the angle iron to be issued to 126 Division Locating Battery as training stores on payment. He also issued a cheque towards the payment of these stores.

Captain AK Kher was left off after a heavy dose of firing and the rest of the tenure was incident-free.

Sikkim later became a part of India in early 1975 following a Referendum.

□

VOLUME III

OPERATION MEGHDOOT, 1984
HIGHEST BATTLEFIELD
IN THE WORLD

19
The Place of Roses

Siachen in the Balti language means, '*sia*' as 'rose' and '*chen*' as place of".

The Karachi pact in 1949, mediated by the UN and signed by the military representatives of India and Pakistan, had established a ceasefire line in Kashmir following the Indo-Pak war of 1947. The line between the two nations was demarcated up to the point NJ980 420 at the foot of the Siachen Glacier, in the extreme north of both the countries.

The glacier from the terminus point of 11,875 feet above sea level extends to its highest point at 18,875 feet above sea level. The inhospitable terrain beyond point NJ9842 (point as referred to by India and Pakistan) was obviously not demarcated, simply because UN officials did not think that either country would ever dispute such a barren region where the average temperature is -15 degrees throughtout the year and dips to -50 degrees in the winters and where the average snowfall is 35 feet. But in the decades following the Karachi Agreement, both India and Pakistan claimed sovereignty over the Siachen area.

It is commonly believed that before the conflict started in 1984, the Siachen Glacier had been lying in quiet isolation given the desolation of this region. Such a belief was understandable but not true. The glacier has had many visitors for a long time, both local and foreign since the 1930s.

As the ambiguity about the line of control in this area further remained in the 1972 Simla Agreement too, Pakistan promoted and permitted many foreign expeditions to the Siachen Glacier between 1972 and 1983. These expeditions were accompanied by Pakistani Army personnel. They generally crossed over the Gyong La, Bilafond La or Sia La to enter the glacier area. They climbed and did explorations on most of the peaks, like Teram Kangri, Singhi Kangri and others. These frequent ingresses were the grounds on which Pakistan had laid claim to the glacier on their maps. They even went to the extent of establishing a few military posts as staging points for the expeditions. Some of these posts were also well stocked with tinned rations.

During this period, the Indian Army also sent three expeditions to the glacier. In 1978 there was an expendition led by Col Narendra Kumar, who approached from Nubra Valley and climbed Teram Kangri II. In September 1980, an expedition led by Brigadier KN Thadani climbed Apsaras I and again in April 1981 an expedition led by Col Narendra Kumar reached the upper glacier and climbed Saltoro Kangri I, Sia Kangri I, Indira Col, Sia La, Turkestan La and Saltoro Pass.

And then, from 1983 onwards, India began receiving intelligence reports warning of Pakistani Army incursion into the region and a potential assault on the Saltoro Ridge–a strategic location on the South-west side of the Siachen Glacier. India preemptively launched Operation Meghdoot on 13th April, 1984 before the Pakistani assault could commence.

246 Mountain Regiment, with newly inducted 105 mm Indian Field Guns, was deployed at Nubra Valley base camp area before the commencement of Infantry operations.

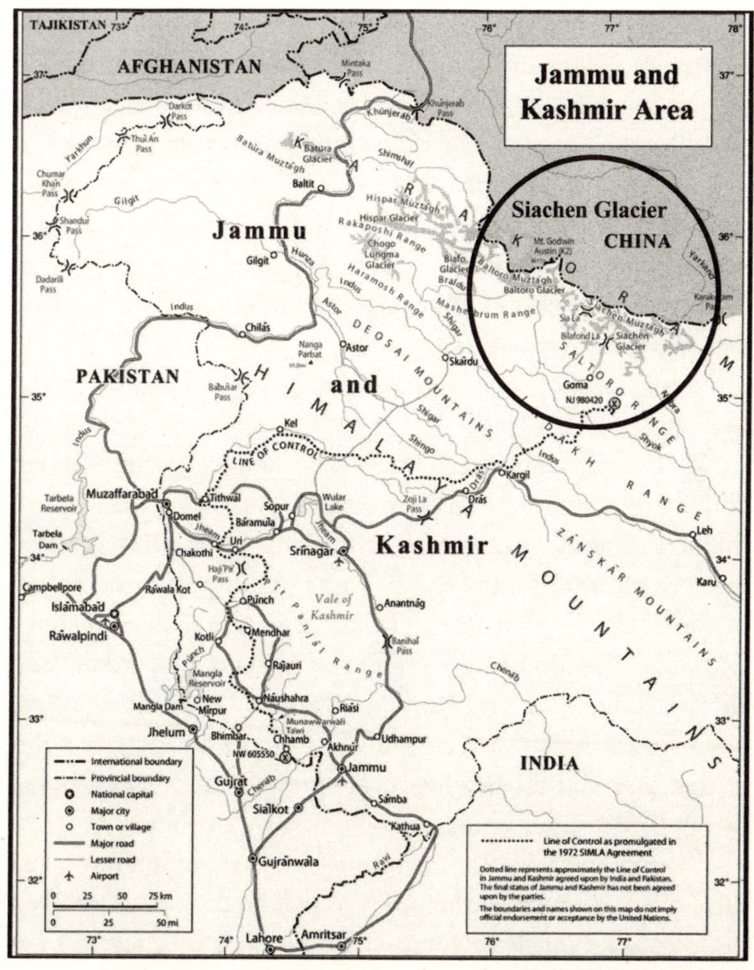

MAP NO 3953 REV 4 UN

A taskforce was set up and it was headed by Lt Col Pushkar Chand and with him were troops of the special Ladakh Scouts led by Major Ajay Bahuguna and 4 Kumaon troops led by Major RS Sandhu. The Indian Army moved in at lightning speed in a race to occupy the Saltoro Heights.

The urgency was such that on inaccessible heights, the troops of 4 Kumaon in a helicopter-borne operation landed on the glacier. Cheetah helicopters of 114 Helicopter Unit could carry only two men at maximum and were operating at its highest service ceiling. At least 30 sorties were conducted to induct troops. These troops did not have specialised protection gear against the cold as limited equipment existed for such an operation. They had less ammunition and almost no Administrative backing.

Upon landing, they set up small posts and camps on the glacier.

Pakistani Heli reconnaissance noticed the Indian deployment and its Northern Light Infantry (NLI) of 62 Infantry Brigade along with SSG troops was alerted. They were constituted as the Burzil Force and now started racing towards the heights under Operation code name Ababeel, with the intention of vacating any Indians and taking the Saltoro Ridge. But by 17th and 18th April, 1984, the Indian Army had already taken control of around 1,000 square miles of territory and the Siachen Glacier was effectively occupied by our brave men against all odds.

The troops used for operations were mountain boys who did not need much acclimatisation and could live on smoked yak meat and *thookpa*. By the time the Pakistanis arrived, the Indians had already captured the heights of Saltoro and were well entrenched. On 25th April, 1984, the first armed clashes took place on Siachen when a Pakistani patrol opposite Bilafond La attacked the 4 Kumaon Post with small arms fire. This attack was repulsed with heavy casualties inflicted on the enemy.

India was now in control of the Siachen Glacier and all its tributary glaciers as well as all the main passes and ridges of the Saltoro. Meanwhile the enemy went on to occupy positions at the lower elevation of Gyong La, Yarma La and access route to K2.

On 20th June, 1984, the enemy once again set out to launch an attack on the Indian Post at Bilafonda La. L/Nk Chanchal Singh of 4 Kumaon was sadly killed on 23rd June by enemy HMG fire becoming the first casualty caused by the Pakistanis. This time the enemy was engaged by the Field Guns of 246 Mountain Regiment which not only decimated the attack, but the enemy also had to vacate their defensive post of Ali Brangsa. During the rest of the 1980s and throughout the 1990s, the enemy side launched various combat operations in an attempt to take strategic positions.

Thus a new front was opened between India and Pakistan which is now the world's highest battlefield where the following challenges have to be first overcome on a daily basis, even before facing the enemy. Most fatalities have been due to the severe conditions at the high-altitude glacier rather than enemy bullets.

High Altitude Sickness

Troops from the plains need a three-stage acclimatisation for induction and a period of 20 days is needed for that.

Pulmonary Edema

Due to the lack of oxygen, the lungs get filled with water and unless evacuated to lower altitude immediately, death is a certainty.

Cerebral Edema

The brain swells with fluids and immediate evacuation to lower altitude is necessary.

Retinal Haemorrhaging

Due to exposure to direct sunlight in the rarefied air, the wearing of snow goggles is mandatory.

Hypothermia and Frostbite

Body temperature falls dangerously low. Severe damage of tissue due to formation of ice crystals within the cells takes place. The cells are ruptured and die and ultimately amputation of the affected part becomes necessary.

Hyper Acidity

One has to be very careful with the quality of food; it has to be mild in *masalas* and cooked in butter and be nutritious. Blood vomiting is a common symptom and Tibetan *thookpa* is the best food recommended on the high mountains.

Hygiene and Sanitation

Also very complicated is bathing and changing of clothes which is only possible once you come down after a minimum three months' rotation and if you happen to wash your orifices with ice-cold water, instant blisters occur and imagine the plight of a blighter who has a blister on his.....

Cooking

Due to lack of air pressure, everything comes to a boil, but nothing actually gets cooked and forces have to depend on poor-quality tinned stuff.

Last but not the least, the impact of the weather is on the weapons which do not fire or their parts break off after short use.

Above are the factors which have to be first tolerated and if that does not get to you, then the enemy gets an opportunity to take a shot. The glacier itself has a much higher killing score than the enemy as of date, making this battle very unique and every individual who has served or is serving the country in this area must be awarded a place of honour among the countrymen of both sides.

□

20

A Destined Path

Back in 1957 when Major Ashok Kumar Kher was a nine-year old boy, his father Mr. Dwarika Nath Kher got transferred to Leh. At that time he was heading the accounts branch of the Srinagar-Leh Road project and the entire family had to move to Leh.

It was a tough journey on horseback as back then only a mule track existed from Sonamarg to Leh. In between from Baltal to Zoji La Pass, a gravel track of a one-ton vehicle capacity existed but unfortunately no civilian transport existed to utilise this road. Further on the Machoi Glacier existed then, which could only be passed on horseback.

In those days it took the family around two months to reach Leh, crossing a total of three dangerous passes and a glacier. Zoji La, Machoi glacier, Namika La, Fotu La – in that order and this included a break at Kargil for 20 days due to the weather.

About 30 years later, most of the Machoi has melted due to global warming.

In Aug 1984, a Medium troop of three 130 mm guns was moved to Nubra Valley ahead of Leh and deployed at base-camp location for immediate support of Operation Meghdoot. This troop comprised of one gun from each Battery of 39 Medium Regiment with a mixed Command Post staff.

The requirement of OPs on Siachen was large and local units could not cater for it. 401 Independent Artillery Brigade in Jammu was detailed to provide one OP officer for the glacier. 39 Medium Regiment as part of 401 Independent Artillery Brigade provided the under-mentioned officers to serve the glacier as OP officers (a) Captain FS Virk on Bilafond La, (b) Captain MM Yadav also on Bilafond La and (c) Captain RS Galawat on G3 (Pehalwan). Each OP stayed for a period of three months on the glacier and when these bravehearts came down to the unit, their body weight would be three-fourths of their original weight.

On 1st June, 1985, the CO 39 Medium Regiment Col JRK Bhattacharji called for a Battery Commanders' (BC) conference in his office at Basoli Cantonment, Jammu and informed them that the Medium troop deployed at Siachen had to be augmented to one full Battery to enhance the fire power and coverage area.

After hearing the CO out, Major AK Kher, Battery Commander 122 Medium, said that as per tradition, only 122 Medium Battery had been going for independent missions ever since the inception of the unit. Being the senior most Battery Commander, he volunteered for this task. Besides upholding the unit tradition, Major Kher also happened to be a Jammu & Kashmir native, having spent his childhood at Leh. He deemed it his right to defend the native land.

CO Col Bhattacharji, after due consideration, accepted.

122 Medium Battery had six guns out of which one Gun detachment had moved earlier in August 1984 to Nubra Valley base camp and deployed. Major Kher handed over one gun each internally to other Batteries (123 and 393 Medium) and was to take over the two guns already deployed at Nubra of 123 and 393 Medium Battery. Those along with the remaining

three guns of 122 Medium Battery, would make up a complete Medium Battery at Siachen.

On 10th June, 1985, Major AK Kher had his orders, three guns of 122 Medium Battery to move from Basoli to Udhampur-base workshop for dismantling and for further proceeding to Partapur base camp. In Udhampur-base workshop, each gun was taken apart and loaded in four *Shaktiman* vehicles of three-ton capacity. Barrel in one, Recoil in second, Legs in third, Cradle and Bogey in fourth. All the parts were securely lashed and fixed by nuts and bolts and brackets. This operation took about five days to be accomplished.

Disassembly of guns at Udhampur workshop

122 Medium Battery at Udhampur ready to move

Col JRK Bhattacharji came to Udhampur to see off 122 Medium Battery and a convoy of one jeep, one 1-ton, 17 Shaktimans and one Kraz which were ready to move to Srinagar. The Kraz 255B, which was a new model vehicle from the USSR, was specially added to the convoy. This vehicle was brought in from the Rocket Regiment as 39 Medium had older and less powerful models.

Captain Manmohan Yadav (who had already spent time as OP on Siachen), Captain Arun Singh Rathore, son of former CO Lt Col AS Rathore (15th May, 1972 to 6th October, 1976) with Gunner Subedar Kashmir Singh (Kala) and technical assistant Subedar Gurpal Singh (Khushki) were the other leaders in the Battery with the convoy.

After due preparations and concealment, this convoy of 122 Medium Battery, commanded by Major AK Kher, reached Srinagar.

This being a strategically important move, CC Artillery 15 Corps Brigadier Sapatnekar briefed and explained to Major AK Kher at HQ Badami Bagh the importance of the mission and the general area the guns needed to be deployed at. The enemy, after being beaten at Sia La and Bilafond La, was now trying to infiltrate through the southern glaciers of La Yogma, Urdolep and Korisa which had to be covered by Medium Artillery fire to be deployed by Major Kher at designated Post 9 area.

CC Artillery was also specially delighted to know that Major AK Kher could speak fluent Ladakhi and had spent his childhood at Leh.

Now the convoy, after a day's stay at Srinagar, with a loud war cry of "Bole so nihal, Sat Sri Akal," proceeded towards Partapur, Nubra Valley, approximately a 570 km distance from Srinagar.

After a travel of 80 kms, the convoy reached beautiful Sonamarg at the foothills of the dangerous Zoji La Pass and a halt for the night was necessitated. Early morning the next day, the convoy left Sonamarg and was able to cross the deadly Zoji La Pass via Balatal. They reached Drass, which is also known as the Gateway to Ladakh, without any incidents.

Drass, at 10,760 feet above mean sea level, is the coldest inhabited place in India and the second coldest inhabited area on the Earth, after Oymyakon, a small village in Russia. The minimum temperature in Drass plummets to about –40 degrees Celsius in winters and this gave 122 Medium Battery the chills and a precursor to what was waiting for them at Siachen. The place was extremely stunning, with compelling landscape throughout.

The surrounding mountains were a stark reminder of the 1948 war in which Lt Col Rajinder Singh MVC (BAR) was assigned the nearly impossible task of transporting his 7th Cavalry Regiment, comprising of Stuart tanks, up the indomitable Zoji La Pass to Drass area battleground at 11,000 feet above mean sea level and he succeeded in accomplishing the task in record time. The Kabalis, who were occupying Drass, on sighting the tanks, ran from their defences. This earned Rajinder the nickname 'Sparrow'. Upon retirement from military service, he went on to become a two-time Member of Parliament in 1980 and 1985.

Now the 122 Medium Battery convoy halted for the night at Drass transit camp in Kargil district. The OC (Officer Commanding) transit camp accorded 122 Medium Battery special treatment, knowing that it was going to be only hell above this. The next day was a tough journey with the dangerous passes to overcome.

The journey of the convoy from Drass was about 135 km via Kargil, followed by Namika La to Budhkharbu transit camp, which was their next planned halt. At Kargil, which is about 63 km from Drass, the convoy had a short tea-and-*samosa* break which was hosted by 219 Medium Regiment.

After the break, the convoy proceeded to Namika La which is a high mountain pass in the Himalayas Zaskar Range at about 12,139 feet above mean sea level, along the Srinagar-Leh highway. It is the first of the two high passes between Kargil and Leh; the second pass is even higher, which is Fotu La. Budhkharbu transit camp is situated between the two passes and en route, the Battery met Brigadier Toor, Commander of 3 Artillery Brigade who was travelling back to Kargil from Leh with his family. He was delighted to see the Battery and extended a warm welcome to 122 Medium Battery.

The Battery crossed Namika La Pass incident-free and halted at Budhkharbu transit camp for the night.

Brig Toor and Family *Maj AK Kher*

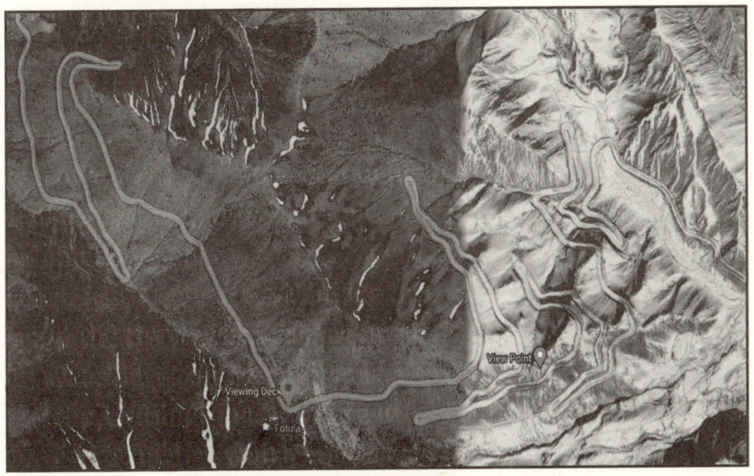

Jalebi Moads after Fotu La (Google Maps)

Early next morning, the convoy proceeded to Fotu La, which hits a high of 13,478 feet above sea level and moving eastwards, the highway begins to descend towards the town of Lamayuru with deadly hairpin bends, known as Jalebi Moad. The convoy crossed the pass – slow, steady and incident free.

Short of Leh is a beautiful village called Nemu which has an old Gompa and beautiful apricot and apple orchards. While the convoy proceeded towards Leh, Major AK Kher stopped briefly and paid homage to Col Hari Chand, his Battalion Commander at OTS in 1968.

Back at the Academy Col Hari Chand was an inspiring figure and his motto was 'time spent in training, digging and patrolling is never wasted'.

In the 1948 war, A Pakistani 3.7 Howitzer was firing from Bosgo village on our advancing column to Ladakh and with Zoji La, Drass and Kargil under enemy control, it was causing critical delay and casualties. Major Hari Chand with his 2/8 Gorkha boys first located and then attacked the enemy gun, destroying it while causing significant casualties and damage to the enemy.

Major Hari Chand was decorated with MVC for his exceptional bravery, initiative and performance.

The convoy reached the famous Gurudwara Pather Sahib, about 25 km short of Leh. 122 Medium Battery offered *ardas, prasad,* did *seva* and prayed for the safety and victory of the mission. In the evening, the convoy reached Leh and halted at Feyang TCP transit camp. Some vehicles needed maintenance, which was carried out.

Meanwhile Major AK Kher went to Karu, the location of HQ 3 Artillery Brigade. At Karu, he met Col Garewal, the Deputy Brigade Commander along with Brigade Major, Major Bhaniwal, who briefed Major AK Kher to deploy guns in area Post 9 just off the map, though none of them had seen, surveyed or made a recce of the area. In a mountainous region, giving a spot off the map for Mediums is unheard of and unprofessional as considerable prior survey work has to be undertaken before setting up a gun area. Post 9 guns were to make sure the enemy did not cut us off from the south side even if the approach was extreamly difficult for the Pakistanis.

Upon returning to Leh from Karu, Major Kher met his childhood friends, visited the house in which his family had stayed in 1957 and thereafter went also to Thiksay Monastery to seek blessings.

The next day from Feyang, Leh the convoy moved towards Partapur sector via the dangerous Khardung La Pass. The convoy approached Khardung La, which is located about 40 km north of Leh and links the capital of Ladakh with the road to the Siachen Glacier.

It is the world's highest motorable Pass at 18,380 feet above sea level. This pass on the Ladakh Range is also the gateway to the Shyok and Nubra valleys. The Siachen Glacier lies part way up the Nubra Valley.

After safely crossing the Pass incident-free on the way to Khalsar, there was a stretch which was totally unpaved rocky road. The convoy suffered 27 tyre bursts. However, Major Kher had forseen this and ensured that the Battery carried the necessary spares.

Hav Bakshi, a veteran from Mule Arty era, drove the Kraz practically on the side of the mountain slope. The vehicle moved with a dangerous tilt.

Only a true Khalsa warrior could drive like this.

Thiksey Monastery above and Google Route Map to Post 9 below

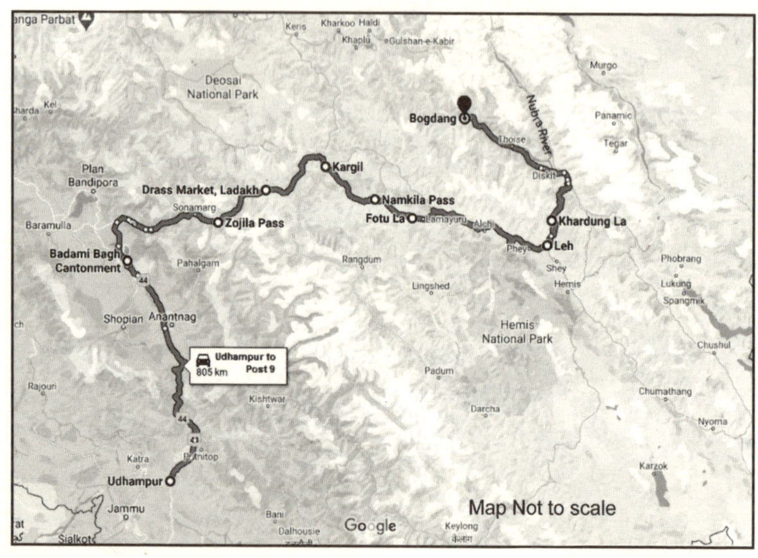

Statue of Maitreya Buddha in Thiksay Monastery

View of Karakoram Range from Khardung La

View of Leh from Khardung La

□

21

Destination Reached

HQ 3 Infantry Division/Trishul Division was located at Leh and responsible for guarding the border with Pakistan from Nubra Valley to Sonamarg and the border with China at Karakoram.

3 Infantry Division was commanded by Maj Gen DD Saklani.

Since 1st March, 1985, Partapur was the location of the newly-established HQ102 Infantry Brigade commanded by Brigadier Jal Master. The protection of Siachen was now upgraded to a full-fledged Brigade level. In the rear of Partapur was Thoise, which has a small strategic airport. Upon reaching Partapur, the gun convoy halted.

Troop A, which had moved in August 1984, was deployed at base camp near the mouth of Nubra river and was about a 10-hour drive from Partapur. Now 122 Medium Battery commanded by Major AK Kher took full charge of the existing 123 and 393 Medium detachments (the third detachment was already of 122 Medium Battery) and all the men of 123 and 393 Medium Battery were now relieved by men of 122 Medium Battery.

Troop A, Base Camp Nubra Valley

Subedar Technical Assistant (TA) Gurpal Singh took over as the Gun Position Officer (GPO) of Troop A, with Nk Tahal Singh being Command Post No 1.

Gun No. 1s of the three detachments were Hav Jaswant Singh, Hav Jarnail Singh and Hav Amarjeet Singh.

BHM was Chhind Singh, who also had the additional responsibility for the Operation Radio Artillery (OPR) and line communication of Troop A.

Base-camp gun position A was at Nubra Valley and gun position B was designated at Post 9 on Diskit-Turtuk Road. Post 9 was about 12 hours' travelling time apart from gun position A with Partapur being much closer to Post 9.

Major AK Kher with Captain MM Yadav and Subedar Kashmir Singh proceeded to recce the Post 9 area for establishing Battery HQ and gun area. Post 9 was about a further two hours' drive on the Diskit–Turtuk Road from Partapur and it was a misnomer to call it even a road as only a narrow gravelled track existed. This track had been lately upgraded for three-ton traffic as it also catered to infantry troops of 18 Kumaon deployed in Turtuk.

The recce party, upon reaching Post 9, was surprised to find no accessible gun area available. On checking with HQ 3 Artillery Brigade at Karu, the great Deputy Commander told Major Kher to deploy the guns on the road itself. But the road had neither the space for a gun nor the crest clearance for 130 mm to be able to fire. It was a big technical issue, which the Deputy Commander had not considered when ordering deployment on the road.

On 22nd June, 1985, Major Kher went back on recce and found a suitable flat ground at Post 9. It was about 150 metres distance from the Diskit–Turtuk Road at a height of 80 degrees gradient but inaccessible by road. An access path had to be constructed for deploying the guns. On return to Partapur, Major Kher met Brigadier Jal Master, the Commander of the 102 Infantry Brigade and requested for Engineer and EME help.

There was no Engineer help as all the dozers were off road and all the help that they could offer was to deploy three men from 435 Engineer Regiment with technical knowledge and a breakdown vehicle (a crane).

Meanwhile CO Col Bhattacharji decided to visit the Battery and Major Kher received him at Leh Airport and drove him over Khardong La, which gave him a good feel of the area and hostility of the terrain. He stayed with the Battery for about two days, visiting the guns at base camp Nubra Valley and the designated Post 9 gun area which was earmarked by HQ 3 Artillery Brigade. After completion of the visit, he flew from Thoise airport itself to Chandimandir.

At Post 9, Major Kher now mustered 122 Medium Battery Khalsas to construct a track to the plateau chosen as Gun Area from the road. It took the Battery about 10 days to construct the track with two major U-turns incorporated to cater to the steep gradient and finally on the 3rd of July, it was complete and ready to receive the gun convoy.

On 4th July, the gun convoy moved from Partapur towards Post 9 Gun Area. The route had narrow twists and turns. The immediate initial challenge encountered was that the Kraz could not negotiate the narrow bridge over a *nullah* which merged with the Shyok river alongside the road and everything came to a halt.

The Shyok river had a depth of about one-metre and a rapid flow and after due consideration, it was decided to drive the Kraz through the river itself instead of over the bridge. But to even accomplish this task, first the Kraz had to be driven down by a 30 to 40 degree gradient to the river-bed. This task was handed to Bakshi, who by reducing air pressure in

KRAZ 255B

the tyres and putting the Kraz in gear 6 × 6 drove it down and across. He did a commendable job and the passage of the Kraz was a success.

But the problems had just begun. The vehicles carrying the barrels of the guns were unable to negotiate the bridge. The barrels were sticking out of the tailboard of the Shaktimans by about one metre and were hitting the rocks jutting over the beginning of the bridge.

After the Kraz had moved across successfully, the decision was made to take the same route for the barrel carrying Shaktimans and using the Kraz winch to secure and move the Shaktiman vehicles across the river. With Bakshi's grit, they were able to cross this obstacle incident-free.

Shaktiman

Upon reaching the spot where the new track was constructed to connect the Post 9 gun area with the highway, Major AK Kher was the first to drive his jeep up and then ordered the breakdown vehicle to follow. Both the vehicles moved up successfully and then the Kraz was ordered to move up, before the gun-carrying vehicles.

Half way up, the track caved in and the Kraz tilted dangerously; Efforts to pull the Kraz up with the breakdown failed. A 500-feet fall and a loss of the new Kraz was imminent and staring at Major Kher.

Now Major Kher was faced with a decision whether to push the Kraz into the *nullah* and write it off or to move the gun convoy up to deploy. Major Kher's jeep driver, Nk Amrik Singh (Rafi) volunteered and requested, "*Sahib manu ik chance do.*" (Sir, give me a chance to drive out the Kraz.) Major Kher agreed and told him to reduce tyre pressure to the lowest level which was a new feature in the 255B-model Kraz and could be done with a switch in the cabin.

The tyres became much broader, giving the Kraz larger traction on the road and securing the remaining wheels on the track. Rafi put 6 × 6 gear after taking Wahe Guru's name and the vehicle shuddered up successfully.

Jubilations all around on this victory. The Kraz was saved and Rafi saved it without worrying for his own life. The track was repaired and now on the 4th of July, the entire fleet was now on the plateau in the newly prepared Gun Area of Post 9.

While unloading the first gun, the breakdown vehicle packed up. Its cables broke and the pulley motor stopped working. So there was no dearth of challenges. The gun in its full firing configuration weighed 7.7 tons. The barrel is mounted on the split tail carriage with deep box section trails and road wheels. At the ends of the split tails, the gun has detachable spades to be fitted when the gun is brought into action.

Now GPO, Subedar Kashmir Singh (Kala) and Gun No 1s of the three detachments – Hav Attar Singh, Hav Hardeep Singh, Hav Harbajan Singh and Gunner Mohinder Singh rose to the occasion and unloaded the guns by using Khalsa muscle power. Each part weighing around two tons needed at least 60 men to lift the barrel. Similar manpower was used to unload other parts of the gun and all the three guns i.e., 21 tons were moved by the team of 60 men and were assembled the same day.

It would be useful to note the difficulty of this task considering the oxygen deprivation at high altitudes. The average altitude of the valley is about 12,000 feet above sea level.

Assembly of Guns at Post 9

Major Kher asked the EME representative to certify the guns fit for firing and they started following the book and saying, "*Shield ka nut bolt nahin ha, kaise certify karaga ji.*" (The shield nut bolt is missing, can't certify.)

There was nothing by the book from the very beginning of this mission and Major AK Kher ordered them to be physically thrown out of the area. He called for Battery gun fitter CHM Ram Singh, and told him, "*Ramay, run out test kar, main recoil and legs' nut bolt check kar.*" (Ram check the run out, main recoil and legs' nut bolts and reply.) CHM Ram Singh after a thorough check then shouted on the mega phone, "Sahib, 122 Medium Battery, B Troop fit for firing."

Troop A was covering the arc from Jwala to Indira Col and Troop B now was covering the southern glacier from Jwala to Gorkha Hill in Turtuk Valley.

On 5th July, 1985, Major AK Kher reported to Brigadier Jal Master of 102 Infantry Brigade, HQ 3 Artillery Brigade and OP at Yash and Jaswant Post, "39 Medium ready to fire."

Gun crew with the sacrificial lamb Troop B Post 9 ready for fire

Terrain Map of Post 9 and Base Camp Gun Position (Google Maps)

□

22

The Day of Reckoning

Post 9 became the highest Medium Gun position in the world now. Post 9 was located in Turtuk Valley.

On 6th July, 1985, Captain Man Mohan Yadav was Gun Position Officer and the OP at Yash, Captain Bhuttia sighted the enemy and ordered the shot: Range 30 km, with charge super and elevation of gun on sights 833 mils and fire. The guns opened up with a loud war cry of *'Jo bole so nihal, Sat Sri Akal'*.

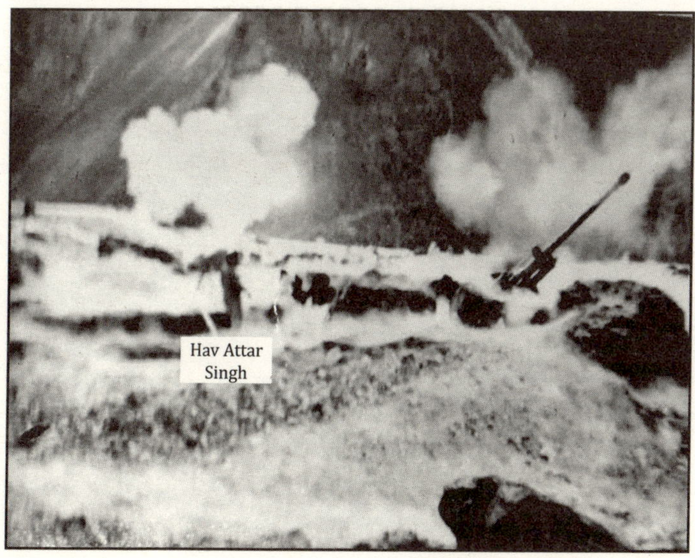

Troop B at Post 9 in action

Six rounds were discharged in a matter of a few minutes and this announced the arrival of 122 Medium Battery.

The ground shook and a glass full of water in Captain Yadav's hand just broke. He told Battery Commander Major Kher, "Sir, this is a good omen."

First there was panic among our Infantry troops as the shells were in flight over them and it made an extremely loud bang, making them think that they were going to explode over them. What they did not know was that the 130 mm gun shell when fired at full charge travels at 1400 feet per second and breaks the sound barrier in flight. This was the sonic boom – that's what caused the overhead loud bang before impacting on the enemy.

Target report was four to five enemy casualties. A second round of salvos was fired on the enemy on the 7th of July, followed by some respite for the enemy till 16th July, when the third round of bombardment took place.

Gun crew with shell and cartridge

The maximum range achieved by 122 Medium Battery was 36 km in the rarefied atmosphere. The Russians had compiled a range table for high altitude for this gun and 39 Medium Regiment was the first to fire a projectile at this range in India.

Just a month ago at the end of May or early June four enemy fighter aircraft had violated Indian airspace, flying over the base camp's defensive positions in Nubra Valley, displaying their intent. The Battery was prepared and could even withstand any aerial or ground attack effectively if it came to that.

The Post had 1,200 rounds of ammo stored in location. The gun area, Command Post, living quarters and cook house were made of strong *sangars*. All the fire trenches were made with *sangars* too.

Supply was poor, as Post 9 was at the end of the supply line. Till lately Turtuk Valley was air maintained due to lack of proper roads. Fresh stock arrived from Srinagar but it was of turnips and knol khol mostly. Fresh water was lifted from the Shyok river directly and somehow the Battery managed it all.

The last northern most Indian village until 1971 was Bugdhan (Bogdang) which was about 3 or 4 km from Post 9 in the Shyok river valley. In the 1971 war, Major Chewang Rinchen MVC (Bar) had captured Chalunka and Turtuk village from Pakistan and extended the Indian boundary beyond Bugdhan up to Gorkha Hill, making Bugdhan comfortably in the interior now. Major Kher went down for liaison and people there were delighted to see him when he spoke to them in Ladakhi. Bugdhan people were Muslims who spoke Ladakhi and wore the Kashmiri *pheran* which was strange as Ladakhis wear the *goncha*. Major Kher was assured of full cooperation from the local villagers.

Turtuk Valley, second Ridge on left is Gorkha Ridge

In Turtuk was the Battalion HQ of 120 Light Regiment and 18 Kumaon Regiment whose troops established the posts like Rewari, Yash, Jaswant, Sadi Saddle, Banshi and Raju Saddle on the southern glacier to dominate the enemy by observation and fire.

18 Kumaon was commanded by Col Mir Fayazuddin, who knew Major Kher from the 1971 operations at Chhamb, the 2 IC was Major GV Katneshwarkar and the Adjutant was Captain Vijay Bahuguna.

Local people at Turtuk spoke Balti and Urdu, but no Ladakhi. They were happy to be part of India. On a visit by Major Kher, the village elders congregated and told him that they had not seen sugar in Pakistani rule and now India was providing them sugar at the same price as in New Delhi. Moreover one person from Turtuk had even gone to Mecca for Haj which had never happened before.

Meanwhile, back at the Nubra base camp, Troop A's N/k Tahal Singh would call every OP officer at glacier in the afternoon and ask for '*haal chaal*' and if they needed anything. Every day he would be at Heli base, sending parcels of dry fruits, cigarettes and mail to various forward OP posts.

After an OP party came down from their forward post rotation, they would stay in 122 Medium Battery Troop A. Only after a shave and bath would they go to their own Regiments. Khalsa hospitality was alive and kicking here also.

N/k Tahal Singh was like Jaspal Bhatti (famous Indian TV comedian) of the unit and a humorous guy. An incident worth mentioning is as follows:

Tahal Singh was on leave, back in Punjab. He was standing in a queue to encash a cheque at the Punjab National Bank.

The teller shouted out, referring to a signature, "Minder Kaur! Minder Kaur *may thera* M (and pronounced it as MAMMA) *nahi melda*, cheque return."

Back in the line, Tahal Singh shouted, "*Bauuji assa karo mera taa sign check karlo, mera* T *tha tatta milda ki nahi*."

Tahal was very quickly called up front and cleared from the bank.

Captain MM Yadav, after successful deployment, went on leave and the Battery was joined by Captain MS Shekhawat as his replacement.

□

23
Call to Enemy

Major Kher, on his regular visit to HQ 102 Glacier Brigade in Partapur, met Commander, Brigadier Jal Master.

The brigadier told Kher that they had spotted three specific enemy targets where a lot of enemy activity was noticed but the forward OPs were unable to engage due to the target locations being complicated. He then wondered if AOP (Air Observation Post) could engage the targets from Rewari sector.

Major AK Kher immediately spotted the problem and said AOP would need at least 20/30 mins. of hover time to undertake a shoot and that's enough for the enemy to bring the chopper down. He further added that OPs in the front were juniors and not experienced enough to effectively engage the complex targets.

Major Kher himself made a decision to move forward and engage the enemy targets personally as only the most experienced OP could do so. Brigadier Jal, himself a paratrooper and a tough Commander, was full of admiration at Major Kher's motivation to observe and engage the enemy and agreed to a senior Battery Commander going up to the post.

Brigadier Jal Master went on to narrate the following incident that had happened a month ago to Major Kher, to explain the intent and determination of the enemy. On 14th June, at about 0900 hrs, he was carrying out a recce by helicopter and noticed that from the enemy side of the saddle, the Pakistanis were climbing up, using ropes. The 18 Kumaon patrol led by CHM Sadi Ram were cooped up in a tent about a km away from the saddle. Brigadier Jal had to urgently get their attention and hovered over the tent before finally managing to convey the important piece of information by dropping two chits on the tent tied to a heavy object. In one of the chit, it was written 'Enemy across the Saddle'; in the other chit, the same thing was written in Hindi. Luckily the chits were collected by CHM Sadi Ram and he acknowledged the message by giving a thumbs up.

CHM Sadi Ram immediately organised his patrol to race up the saddle in waist-deep snow, which was a climb of 80 degrees gradient. It was a race to do or die. The last stretch was a 10 to 12 feet of ice wall and scaling that was important to reach the top. With great effort, N/k Vidya Nand was the first to reach the top with a push from Maukam Singh, who was LMG No 2. Vidya Nand had only enough time to pull up Maukam's LMG with the help of a rope and quickly opened fire on the advancing enemy, resulting in one enemy soldier being killed and a few others injured. The enemy attack was thwarted, saving the saddle from capture and saving the day. Vidya Nand was later awarded the Sena Medal and the saddle was named 'Sadi Saddle' after CHM Sadi Ram.

Upon Brigadier Jal finishing the story, Major Kher proceeded back to Post 9.

On the 23rd July, Major Kher decided to proceed to Yash OP as per plan with his most trusted and faithful radio operator, Anokh Singh, each moving on man-pack basis. The route was extremely difficult with an immediate 8 hour climb up the steep mountain from Post 9 itself, followed by a 4 hour descent to Waris village.

Waris was a self-contained village in this inaccessible area. The people were generally well-to-do and a good area was under cultivation with a lot of *pashmina* goats and yaks. Waris had a small detachment of 18 Kumaon to check for enemy infiltration. Major Kher and Anokh Singh spent the night with them. Next day, Major Kher met the village headman, who was delighted to hear him speak in Ladakhi. The village headman was kind enough to offer his horse to carry the man-packs till the farthest point possible.

Next day, Major Kher and Anokh Singh proceeded towards Rewari base camp located on the glacier. The glacier starts a little ahead of Waris village where they bid adieu to the horseman. The base camp is called Rewari after the brave Ahir men from Rewari area occupied it just before the summer of 1984. All along, Major Kher and his radio operator Anokh walked over moraines, which are made of rocky debris carried along by the melting of snow and ice. All of a sudden, the weather turned and it started to rain.

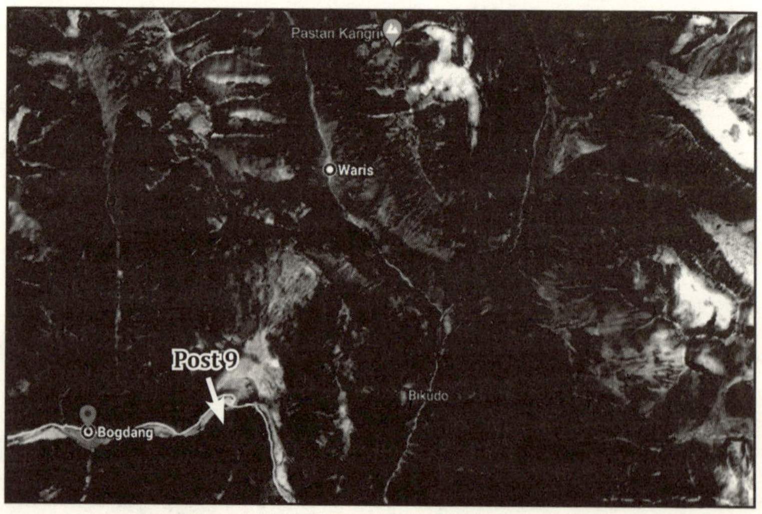

Climb to Waris from Post 9 (Google Maps)

The temperature plummeted and they had no protection. The only alternative available was to open their man-packs and take out the mattress kapok (waterproof on one side), which they wrapped over themselves and moved forward.

Waris Village Camp

By late afternoon, they reached the gunner base on the way and had lunch with them. Then after an hour's ascent, they reached the Rewari base.

Rewari was the company HQ of 18 Kumaon and there the Company Commander, Major BB Thapa was eagerly awaiting Major Kher. 18 Kumaon had organised special clothing and equipment needed at the glacier. After a night's rest Major Kher, Anokh Singh and Major Thapa proceeded to the Observation Post called Yash, which was about an hour's trek further from Rewari base and at 19,500 feet on the crest line of the Urdolep Glacier.

On 25th July, 1985 early in the morning, the party reached Yash OP. Major Thapa pointed out the targets to Major Kher and these were three big *khaddas* (dugouts) where the enemy had their dumps of ammo and rations stored.

The JCO-in-charge of Yash Post briefed Major Kher about the targets being defended by platoon level strength of the enemy. He further informed that a man was seen in white dress who seemed to be the Commander of the enemy post and had a living facility in *Khadda* No 3. The other two dugouts were for ammo and rations. Major Kher proceeded to analyse the target and fully appreciated it. The line of fire from Post 9 passed over Yash OP. The probable zone of impact was 250 meters either side of the target. Major Kher decided to take on the target by precision method and using the single gun with clinometer laying.

Rewari Base Camp

The range of gun to target was 33 km.

The distance from OP to target was 1 km and elevated by at least 2,500 feet.

Radio Operator, Anokh Singh relayed Major Kher's orders to the GPO at Post 9 gun area to fire. The GPO worked the technical data and relayed range, bearing, type of charge and angle of sight. Round one was fired by Gun detachment No. 1 of Hav Attar Singh and it was a target round. Major Kher made slight adjustments in the line and range and ordered firing of 20 more rounds.

During the shooting, accidentally one round landed very close to the OP position. Fortunately it went deep inside the snow and did not explode.

Rewari

From his vantage point at Yash, Major Kher observed that all the three *khaddas* had rounds landing on top of them. The shells of 130mm each, weighing *ek mun* (76 lb) caused chaos and total destruction to the enemy.

Gun Fire

The man in white clothes was never seen again. All the enemy movement in this area was halted and all the threats emanating neutralised.

Major Kher announced a peg over the radio to the Battery for the successful shooting.

Enemy radio intercept later confirmed casualty figures as including one officer, 12 other ranks killed, eight injured and all ammo and ration dumps destroyed.

After nearly wiping out the enemy platoon by accurate shooting, Major Kher, Anokh Singh and Major Thapa came back to Rewari base and rested for the night.

The Shell that fell too close to Yash Op

□

24
Judgement Day

Jaswant post at 22,000 feet above sea level is the most dominant locality in Rewari area (Korisa Glacier), which is the southern part of the Siachen Glacier. This was manned by a High Risk Mission officer, Captain Rathi with an Artillery OP officer, Captain Amarjeet Singh and Sub Jaswant Singh along with troops from 18 Kumaon Regiment. This position was dominating and important for the defence of the entire Rewari complex. NJ 9842 was 3 or 4 km south of this location.

Major Kher had planned to visit Jaswant Post from the onset, which was about four to five hours' climb up from the Rewari base. On 26th July, 1985 early in the morning, Major Kher, his radio operator Anokh Singh, along with N/k Subey Singh Yadav, a guide from Major BB Thapa's A Coy, set out for Jaswant Post.

Anokh Singh with Major Kher and N/k Subey Singh Yadav

It was an audacious climb over crevasses and the area was avalanche-prone. Negotiating the challenges of the terrain, by late noon they reached Jaswant Post. Originally Pakistanis used the Jaswant Post as a staging area for their expeditions. It was usually vacated in winters by the enemy. Subedar Jaswant Singh Yadav lead a team of 18 Kumaon and occupied this feature before the Pakistanis could come back and hence the the Post was named Jaswant Post.

Major Kher and his team were welcomed with a hearty lunch on arrival and were fed some Pakistani rations captured by Sub Jaswant Singh. Both the officers at the Post were happy to welcome Major Kher because he was a senior Artillery Battery Commander visiting Jaswant. Usually all senior visitors normally turned back from Rewari base.

Thereafter Major Kher studied the enemy position in detail. He further learnt from Captain Rathi that on any visible movement, the enemy would fire mortars to pin the troops down at the post. Captain Rathi further indicated the approximate position of the enemy Observation Post from where the mortar fire was directed.

Major AK Kher with Capt Amarjeet Singh and Capt Rathi at Jaswant Post

This Post was so critical that at night, one officer would always stand on watch duty. Both Captain Rathi and Captain Amarjeet Singh used to take turns to stand guard. Despite coughing blood, Captain Rathi would continue to stand guard at the post for God and Country. He never complained.

A special mention must be made of Anokh Singh's character, grit and determination. Upon learning that the enemy reacted with mortar fire on this Post, Anokh was asked by Major Kher to stay in adm base which was safer. Anokh was too young to die or get injured. But Anokh refused, "Sahib I will not leave you alone and will not obey such instructions. God forbid, if something happens to you, back at the base men will tear me to shreds for leaving you alone to face the enemy." Major Kher just bowed his head to Anokh in sheer respect.

Early next morning, on 27th July, Major Kher laid down his plan. Anticipating a full-blown enemy reaction, Jaswant Observation Post area was cleared. All excess men moved to safer positions but constantly kept the enemy under watch.

Major Kher, along with Captain Rathi and Captain Amarjeet, moved to the observation position with Anokh manning the communications. The first target was enemy-defended locality and once again Major Kher used the single-gun precision method to target the enemy.

Range of gun to target was 32 km

OP to target was 1 km

Height of target and OP was the same.

Since the impact zone of the gun was too large, it was rather difficult to effectively get rounds to land on target. Major Kher took some time to appreciate the target. As the apex angle was large the zone started playing on his mind. However, using his experience, Major Kher relayed precise fire orders to the GPO and the Gun detachment No. 2 of Hav Hardeep Singh effectively engaged the enemy locality and scored direct hits.

Major Kher's second shoot was on a suspected position of the enemy's Observation Post. He again used the single-gun precision method to neutralise the target and scored direct hits.

Now the enemy, in response, opened up with 120 mm mortars. They had American-made super quick fuses which burst immediately on impact with snow and the splinter effect was all round, and very effective. The enemy retaliatory firing lasted for about 30 to 40 mins. The protective measures worked and no major damage was done on to the Jaswant Post.

Major Kher, originally being a counter-bombardment specialist, used his extensive knowledge to locate the enemy mortar position. It was at extreme range and around the most northern spot from where the marked NJ 9842 would end, if an imaginary line was drawn to absolute north of Saltoro.

The range of gun to target was 36 km

Twice, while giving corrections, GPO replied that the range was expended.

Gun Loading

Gun Fire

Major Kher ordered fire with charge super and multiple rounds were discharged. Enemy mortar fire stopped, to the jubilation of the boys at Jaswant Post.

In total, approximately 60 shells were fired at the enemy for about three hours. During this shoot, 39 Medium earned the distinction of firing 130 mm gun projectiles to a range of 36 km which was the maximum ever achieved in India until then.

After a good celebratory lunch at Jaswant Post, Major Kher and Anokh moved back to Rewari base. The sun was up and so was the temperature. At this height, movement is very slow and the people get out of breath within a short period of time which is very common. The time taken for descent was much greater than that taken for going up.

Due to the sun being up in the afternoon the snow cover had become much softer. Anokh, being light, could move but Major Kher's every step started sinking in. Now crevasses became visible and it was frightening to see the depth to which they extended. During Major Kher's college days, he had learned about ice craft and had climbed Buttress Peak, which is next to Kolohoi Peak in Kashmir and this experience came in handy during the descent.

At places, Major Kher had to take the lying position to avoid sinking and make swimming movements to cross soft patches of snow. During the descent, the team faced three avalanches, rocks and loose ice chunks coming down on them, but fortunately missing by a few metres. The team reached Rewari base, thoroughly exhausted and stayed there for a couple of days. Air observation team of 662 OP Sqn was kind enough to send two choppers for them. Major Kher and Anokh were airlifted back to Partapur, from where they went to Post 9, 122 Medium Battery HQ.

Climb down from Jaswant

□

25

Return to Jubilations

After a few days, the Commander of 102 Glacier Brigade visited 122 Medium Battery. He was gracious enough to bring a few cases of rum for the Battery and he addressed a *sammelan*. He told the Battery that while travelling to location, he too climbed the track made by the 122 Medium Battery's self-effort and fully realised that the Khalsas had brought India's biggest gun to an impossible area. He said he was proud to have 122 Medium Battery in his brigade and specially thanked the Battery Commander, Major AK Kher for his shooting exploits from the glacier.

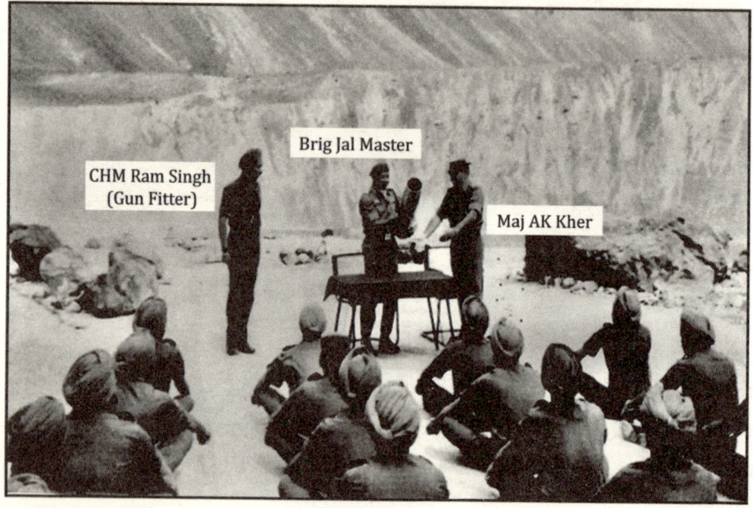

Post 9

Brig Jal Master with Capt MS Shekhwat and Gun No. 1

On 10th August, 1985, a Cheetah helicopter was seen hovering above 122 Medium Battery gun area and the pilot was making some signs. The gun position had no helipad, nor did Major Kher have any intimation of any choppers coming their way. Major Kher was a bit surprised and directed the Cheetah to a flat spot where it landed safely.

Out came a senior gentleman wearing a *parkha* and a Gorkha hat. He asked Major Kher what the hell he was doing there. Major Kher, in his customary style, said, "I am here to fuck the enemy, and that is exactly what I am doing here."

The pilot knew Major Kher for his verbose expressions from previous meetings and came in quickly. He told Kher that he was talking to the Officiating GOC Brigadier Raj Kumar Suri, VrC who himself was a decorated officer. Brigadier Suri then as Lt Col had earned his VrC for the 1971 operations while commanding 4 JAT in the Fazilka sector.

Major AK Kher immediately gave a stand fast to Medium Battery and in a customary 'take post' position, gave an official report about guns, ammo, communications and administration.

Meanwhile, the Khalsas brought in sizzling hot *pakoras* with hot tea, which was a speciality of Nk Rajbir Singh, the cook.

They settled down next to the Battery Commander's hut. Brigadier Suri told Major Kher that he was there to investigate a diplomatic protest lodged by Pakistan. He further said that on 27th July, the Battery had engaged a target on the demarcated border NJ 9842 and caused considerable damage of men and material to Pakistan.

Brigadier Suri asked for Major Kher's comments at which Major Kher stood by the events and his conduct on the glacier.

Brigadier Suri got up and shook Major Kher's hand and congratulated him on his fine shooting exploits. The Brigadier informed them that the shooting had killed one officer and 17 other ranks, destroying their post and dumps. This information was verified by Division HQ via the enemy's radio intercepts.

The brigadier assured the Battery of full support and made a note of the problems that existed and later issued effective instructions to solve them. Till October, normal activities of engaging targets from both Troop A and B continued and Major Kher would shuttle between the two locations, looking after the men and keeping them motivated so that their morale remained at an all-time high.

The administration at the base camp Troop A was top-notch. The Battery Commander on each stay was fed *kaleji* with *paratha* for breakfast and fresh goat meat for dinner on regular basis. Army Supply Corps seldom issued meat on hoof.

On enquiry it was found that Troop A had a she-goat that was very well fed and looked after. She was used as a bait to attract the he-goats of the neighbouring units and once the goat came into troop A area, it would vanish. The remains were buried in a well dug under a sentry post and covered with wooden planks. Hav Chhind Singh was the man responsible for the top adm *bandobast*.

On way to Nubra Valley Base camp Troop A

Major AK Kher was scheduled to fly with AOP for an observation mission over the main glacier. Major Kher had tied up with the two chopper pilots of 662 Air OP Squadron – Major SK Gadhok and Captain Gularia for the 30th August sortie. Upon reaching the ALG and about to board the chopper, the weather packed up and the pilots informed Major Kher that he would not be able to observe the glacier or the ridge due to poor visibility and was advised to wait for it to clear.

The AOP flew on their routine sortie and withen 10 mins the chopper was back, emitting heavy smoke. Sadly the chopper got an LMG burst from the enemy which Major Suresh Kumar Gadhok took directly to the head. The enemy had managed to scale a mountain peak, aimed and fired at the chopper, immediately taking Major Suresh Kumar Gadhok down and damaging the chopper. Captain Gularia was able to land, showing tremendous skill and courage. Major Suresh Kumar Gadhok was posthumously awarded the Shaurya Chakra.

On 18 September, CO Col JRK Bhattacharji visited the Battery and Major Kher was informed that in October a

Cheetha Helicopter

Battery of 217 Medium Regiment would relieve 39 Medium Regiment's 122 Medium Battery. The process was to hand over the guns of both Troop A and B to 217 along with the Kraz and take over 217's guns at Basoli, Jammu. Major Vijay Gupta came in as Major Kher's replacement for taking over. As usual, the Khalsas accounting was poor and it was found while handing over ammunition that one box of fuse HE 231 was deficient (diffy in Khalsa language).

Unfortunately, Vijay turned out to be a by the book *kanuni* (lawful) guy and he refused to accept any liability. Major Kher took the Battery charge back from Vijay and asked the OP to take a shoot. Six shells had their exploders removed, the base plugs tightened one by one, loaded and fired. Six fuses now stood expended by the book. And now Major Kher handed over the Battery with no deficiency to Vijay. Major Vijay was aghast at the process employed to overcome the deficiency and became very cooperative. He took over the command of the Battery.

Captain Rathore said to Battery Commander Major Kher, "Sir, Khalsaji, *hisab kitaab* can get you in serious trouble." Major Kher, "They are my men and I have to stand by them, but I advise you not to do such a thing."

On 1st November, 1985, after an eventful deployment at Siachen, 122 Medium Battery moved out.

Maj Vijay Gupta 217 Med Regiment with Maj AK Kher

कर्नल बी पी सिंह
कमान अफसर
Col B P Singh
Commanding Officer

(173) २१९ मध्यम रेजीमेंट
द्वारा ५६ ए पी ओ
219 Medium Regiment
C/o 56 APO

(184)

308701/ 116 /A

01 Nov 85

My dear Colonel,

1. I am taking the liberty of writing to you on behalf of Cdr 102 Inf Bde and Cdr 3 Arty Bde and to convey to you their appre for a very fine performance put up by your gallant boys of 122 Med Bty in "OP MEGHDOOT".

2. The fire sp provided was always timely and accurate which speaks volumes of the std of unit. I am sure you will convey these sentiments to them at an appropriate moment.

With warm regards
Yours sincerely
BP

Col JRK Bhattacharjee
CO
39 Med Regt
c/o 56 APO

Reply

m	RK
185

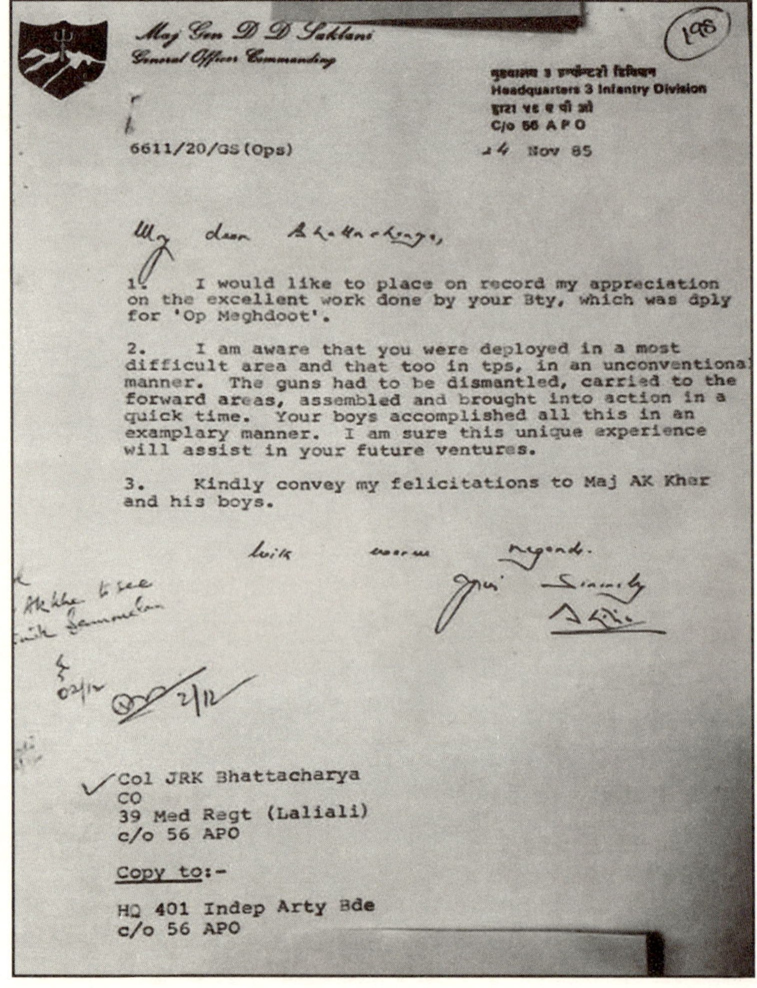

Maj Gen D D Saklani
General Officer Commanding

मुख्यालय 3 इन्फेन्टरी डिविज़न
Headquarters 3 Infantry Division
द्वारा ५६ ए पी ओ
C/o 56 APO

6611/20/GS(Ops)

24 Nov 85

My dear Bhattacharya,

1. I would like to place on record my appreciation on the excellent work done by your Bty, which was dply for 'Op Meghdoot'.

2. I am aware that you were deployed in a most difficult area and that too in tps, in an unconventional manner. The guns had to be dismantled, carried to the forward areas, assembled and brought into action in a quick time. Your boys accomplished all this in an examplary manner. I am sure this unique experience will assist in your future ventures.

3. Kindly convey my felicitations to Maj AK Kher and his boys.

With warm regards.

Yours Sincerely

Col JRK Bhattacharya
CO
39 Med Regt (Laliali)
c/o 56 APO

Copy to:-

HQ 401 Indep Arty Bde
c/o 56 APO

कर्नल वी के बहुगुणा, सेना मेडल
कमान अधिकारी
Col V K Bahuguna, S M
Commanding Officer

18 बटालियन कुमाऊँ रेजिमेन्ट
द्वारा 56 ए पी ओ
18th Battalion The Kumaon Regiment
C/o 56 A P O

LIVE DANGEROUSLY

121/5(SJ)/PRI | 16 Dec 2000

My dear Kher Sir,

1. On the momentous occasion of battalion's Silver Jubilee, Siachen and Sri Lanka warriors fondly remember our association in Op Meghdoot during 1985.

2. The shell presented by you to the bn always reminds us of our association. I am sure you will make an effort to grace this joyous occasion.

Hope you remember me. I was doing adjt. It will be pleasure if you can make it.

With warm regards

Yours sincerely

Vijay

Lt Col A.K. Kher
Adm Regt
School of Arty
Devlali

26

De-induction of 122 Medium Battery

After handing over both A and B gun troops of 122 Medium Battery, the full Battery assembled at Khalsar transit camp. The loads of the two troops were redistributed and balanced. Preparations were made for crossing the dreaded Khardung La Pass for the onward journey to Leh. It was the month of November and winter had set in. The night spent at Khalsar transit camp was cold.

Early next morning, Captain Rathore reported to Battery Commander Kher that men were carrying high-altitude rations in their packs. This was unauthorised and unwarranted and after earning name, respect and fame Major Kher did not want this blot on the Battery.

Battery Commander Major AK Kher ordered a kit layout of all ranks. All high-altitude rations were confiscated and handed over to OC transit camp. This delayed the move till noon but the Battery left the area with its record untarnished.

It had started snowing as the convoy was climbing the pass. A km short of Khardung La, a 4 x 2 three-ton of General Reserve Engineer Force (GREF), which was ahead of 122 Medium Battery convoy, got stuck. It started slipping and blocking the road. All efforts to move the GREF vehicle did not succeed. As the day wore on, the temperature dropped to sub zero. To make matters worse, the Battery had handed over snow-clothing and was wearing only light woollens. Major Kher, in his jeep, somehow managed to cross this GREF vehicle and went to the TCP of Khardung La Pass in order to get help for extracting the convoy. As night had fallen, the TCP pleaded helplessness. The Battery was now stuck on the road for the night with snow falling and no help in sight.

The men spent the night keeping warm on hot tea in their vehicles and had only dry rations for food. In the morning, vehicles would not start as the water in their radiators had frozen and most of the engine safety valves had burst. The convoy was now stranded till noon when it became warmer and the frost started to melt. One Shaktiman of 122 Battery managed to cross the block and then was able to tow the GREF truck up the pass, and thus the whole convoy was able to move and reach Leh.

At Leh, Major Kher's company-mate from Officer Training School (OTS), Major Verma was in command of the field workshop. He put all his manpower at the disposal of Major Kher to make 122 Medium convoy vehicles roadworthy for the long journey ahead. The convoy was forced to take two days' maintenance break before moving to Srinagar.

After leaving Leh, the convoy halted at Gurudwara Pather Sahib, where 122 Medium Battery advance detachment had arrived before hand and set up a small function. The Battery thanked and made obeisance to Guru Baba Nanak for bestowing the Battery with respect, name, fame and victory.

Maj Kher with Capt Arun Singh Rathore at Khalsar transit camp

The Battery had *ardaas, langar* and did *seva* in a very big manner, thanking God for bringing back the Battery safe with *fateh* (victory).

The next halt was Budhkharbu transit camp, where the convoy spent the night. The following day, the convoy moved to Drass and rested for the night at a transit camp. Early next morning it finally left for Srinagar.

On reaching Kangan, 30 km short of Srinagar, Major Kher found the road blocked by a huge agitated crowd and the entire convoy came to a standstill. Major Kher moved forward and enquired from the crowd the reason for the blockade. He was informed that an army vehicle had hit a man and crippled him. They would not let the convoy move unless due compensation was paid. 5 Dogra regiment was also moving out and there were many other unit vehicles also in the convoy.

Major Kher pacified the crowd by speaking in local Kashmiri and assured them that he would take suitable action and that the convoy should be allowed to move. They trusted Major Kher's word and allowed movement. They suspected a flagged vehicle was the culprit. Major Kher found one such vehicle and took it to the Corps of Military Police (CMP) HQ at Badami Bagh.

The Corps HQ ordered an enquiry and the 122 Medium convoy had to halt at Srinagar to assist in the investigation. The CMP Colonel was a thorough professional. He visited the accident site and picked up some glass pieces of the vehicle's headlight found on the spot. He zeroed in on the Mandir vehicle of 5 Dogra and found the broken headlight of the vehicle matched the sample he had collected from the accident site. After the investigation was completed, 122 Medium Battery convoy was allowed to leave Srinagar. Fortunately from Srinagar to Basoli the movement was smooth and incident-free.

Upon reaching Basoli, Jammu 39 Medium Regiment was packing to move to Alwar, Rajasthan.

□

VOLUME IV

HUMOUR IN UNIFORM

(Caption from *Reader's Digest*)

27

Anecdotes

During one of the live fire-training exercises on the ranges, CO Lt Col Gopal Singh indicated a target to the Observation Post (OP) officer for engagement. The OP Captain Sultan Mahmood shouted, "Target not seen." The CO lay the cross hair's of director instrument on target. Captain Mahmood reported again, "Not seen." The CO got angry, "Okay, Mahmood, man-pack your OP party, move in the direction as indicated." This was even while the firing continued, "When you reach the target, I will tell you on wireless" (radio). Captain Mahmood started moving towards the target area, while the other OP's continued shooting in the target area.

Lt Col Gopal Singh VrC,
Zabardast old Fauji

Gopal was *zabardast*, so was Mahmood fearless.

The CO would usually be dressed in khaki shorts, PT shoes without socks and no T-shirt. He would run the regimental parades as per his watch and was a stickler for time. Regimental Hav Major (RHM) would be always in his uniform, even in bed, to meet the CO's expectations.

For the Lohri festival day, the Singhs requested a day off.

At 0400 hrs, the CO, in PT dress, appeared in RHM's tent and asked him, "What time is it?"

RHM, "0400, sahib!"

The CO, "No it is 0640 hrs; what will you do now?"

RHM, "*Shreeman Regiment ko PT kay leeye fall in karoonga.*"

All officers and men were on PT parade at 0415 hrs without any cribbing. The CO took the report.

The CO, shouted to all the ranks, "From my position, there will be active enemy MMG fire in coming. I want you all to reach me alive. No casualties."

All officers, JCOs and men crawled and reached his location.

Mind you, the previous day it had rained heavily. The CO was pleased and announced Lohri celebrations for 24 hrs. (*24 ghanta jetna pee sukte ho shaklo.*)

The CO was banned from using the jeep on his own by the Brigade Commander since couple of incidents of drunk driving had resulted in some jeeps of the regiment being unfortunately written off.

So a dispatch rider mounted on a Royal Enfield motorcycle (DR) would drop the CO to the office. One day the CO came to office on a motorcycle, riding himself and the DR had gone missing.

Search parties were sent to locate the DR who had gone to fetch the CO, but no traces of the DR were found. The story emerged that in reality the DR Singh had reported 5 min. late to the CO. The DR had tried to be clever and had manipulated the watch by 5 min. and tried to defend himself for the delay. The CO, annoyed, ordered him to climb the nearest tree. Driver Singh was on top of the tree for the whole day. Mrs Gopal Singh was a magnanimous lady and asked the DR to come down and have some food and water. However, the DR Singh refused the offer. He told her, "*Memsahib, maa CO Sahib ka hukum nahie tod sakta, Jo bhejna hai upar bhejo.*" In the evening, DR Singh was traced on the treetop and after due authorisation, brought down.

The CO liked well turned-out men, who would salute smartly and march elegantly. Generally when he would be on rounds, men would hide lest they may be caught on the wrong foot and get punished. He hated stray dogs on the regimental campus; anybody who wanted a prize from him would produce a dead dog.

The CO was fond of shooting pigeons. He would always have a loaded .22 rifle in his office. Once a big rough, consistent offender was marched up to the CO. The man was begging the Adjutant and SM not to march him to the CO as he feared being shot.

RHM shouted, "No. 113132 gunner AAA Singh charged under Army Act Section 39b, *tez chal thumb*, salute." (Walk fast, stop, salute.)

At the very same time, the CO saw pigeons flying. He picked up his .22 and shot a pigeon. Gunner AAA Singh shat in his pants and fainted. A horizontal AAA Singh was dragged out of the CO's office. AAA Singh was revived but he refused to believe for many days that he was actually alive.

CO's best friend was the barber Dalu Ram, who would give him all the *langar gupshap* (gossip). If ever young officers found Dalu Ram around their quarters, it meant the CO had noticed a bad hair cut. One had no choice but to oblige Dalu Ram, otherwise your OP/GPO party would be man-packing for a 20-mile march.

A man-pack meant (1) Radio 20 kg (2) Battery 30 kg (3) Cable 5 km (4) Plus charging set and extra battery.

CO Lt Col Gopal Singh, VrC, commanded 39 Medium Regiment from 31st October, 1962 to 13th August, 1965.

Deployment of a Mule Artillary Unit

In mountainous terrain due to lack of roads, guns, howitzers and mortars were carried by mules which were known as Mule Arty. The handlers were known as Driver Mule Arty (DMA).

A single Battery mule convoy extended upto 1 km, a full Regiment convoy consisted of approximately 1,000 mules.

Mountain guns could be dismantled or assembled in minutes; each gun would be carried by five mules, with each mule carrying barrel, cradle, recoil, two carriage legs. Ammunition mules were separate. The officers and JCOs had horses as their mounts.

Gun Deployment

A Gun group was the mules' carrying command post and six guns of the Battery.

The main body was all ammo-carrying mules, rations of mules and men along with the *langar* party.

The recce group would consist of the gun position officer of Lieutenant rank, two technical assistants and battery subaltern – all mounted on horses.

Short of the designated gun area, all gun groups would halt at a rendezvous area.

A recce group would gallop to the gun area for a search and to check the various parameters of gun position. Once satisfied, the GPO in gallop would then plant six flags, indicating gun platforms and would also mark Command Post and Director Position. He would then indicate wagon lines (animal lines) which would be 400 or 500 yards to the flank or rear of gun positions.

The GPO would give crisp orders for deployment.

The Battery subaltarn would gallop back to the rendezvous area to fetch the gun group. On seeing the subaltern, the gun group would gallop to gun position at top speed. DMAs, unable to keep pace with mules, would be hanging on to the tails of the mules. Many a times, DMAs would be casualties and many *pagdis* would be missing.

Five mules would recognise their gun flags and stand in correct order for unloading and getting guns into action.

After unloading, the BHM would blow his whistle and gallop to animal lines. All mules would gallop behind the BHM at top speed, without any confusion or mix up.

The ammo convoy would now arrive and firing would commence. During shelling, mules would take the lying prone position.

Many horses and Army mules were gallantry-award winners too. Once a General was mauled by a leopard and his horse fought back and brought the injured General safely back to the lines.

On another occasion, a mule had fallen into a deep ravine; no trace was found and it was given up as missing/believed killed. One fine day, it came back to unit lines with an enemy gun loaded on him. Both the animals were decorated.

Badmash Mules

Any mule giving trouble in loading, dropping load, carrying less load or kicking was deemed an offender and would be marched to the Battery Commander. On charge-sheet punishment, the mule would be awarded extra duties with extra load or reduction of rations.

Mule Arty

Gun Assembly

Second Lieutenant AK Kher when just a 20-year old lad

On joining the unit, 127 Div. Loc Battery, in December 1968, after completion of the YO's course at Deolali, subaltern Kher was given the command of Bravo Sound Ranging section. His section had three jeeps, two one-tons and one three-ton, which was unheard of at that time.

The BA (Registration) No. of Second Lt Kher's jeep was—75 and of the second jeep 22. The third jeep was not held and had no BA.—22 BA jeep had a big splinter hole on the dashboard from the 1965 war but was operational. The hole was not covered to keep the memory alive. The three-ton BA No was—12. Unfortunately the No of the one ton has been forgotten.

Major US Narula was the Commanding Officer, Captain CM Verma was the 2IC and an able administrator, Captain Bhaktawar was C Section Commander and Kher's teacher and literally brought Second Lt Kher up in the unit. Second Lt, UC Shrivastava was A Section Commander.

B Section's No. 1 was Hav Lalu Prasad Yadav, Hav PS Nanaiahya was Command Post No. 1. Recorder Operator Command Post No. 2 was Nk Pande, KC Mittel was the film reader, Shinde was Bokker, Nk Master Singh was SRG Board plotter, L/Nk PK Malik was radio operator, ANT Tanghapan Nair was the Dispatch Rider, Nk Sadashavim, Harbilas and Karam Chand were jeep drivers. Dass was the one-ton driver and Ajay Pal was the three-ton driver. Nk Khem Chand was signal NCO, Ramu Chavan and Ramu Kalabire (killed in action in 1971) were Second Lt Kher's signalmen.

The Sound Ranging operator A section was Hav Subash Command post No. 1 was Hav Madan lal.

In C-section, were Hav KC Dey and Hav Deela Ram

In Battalion HQ, Sub Harnarayan Singh was SJCO while the super efficient BHM was Ramchandar. The JQ was N/Sub Ajit Singh (who was a Kashmiri Sardar from Tral).

Captain AK Kher's Posting at Jalandhar

Captain AK Kher was posted to 20 Locating Regiment at Jalandhar in 1976. Major Surat Singh was Second in Command and was an institution by himself.

A young Surat Singh was studying in DAV College, Jalandhar. One day, while going to college on his cycle, there was a police *naka* at a crossing. The Head Constable blew his whistle and directed Surat to stop. Young Surat Singh ignored the constable and moved ahead. The inspector on *naka* got furious and rushed after him on his motorcycle. After a brief chase the inspector held on to the carrier of Surat Singh's cycle and forcibly stopped him.

The inspector questioned him, "Why did you not obey the signal of the constable? You look to be a gentleman from a good family. What is wrong with you?"

Surat Singh, "Sir, I am a student of BA in DAV College. I heard the whistle of the constable but could not obey him even though I wanted to. I have to thank you for stopping me by holding my cycle carrier as my cycle does not have any brakes."

After a rebuke, the inspector let him go.

Captain Kher's Battery officer, Captain Mohabbat Singh one day was late for the PT parade. He was called to Captain Kher's office for an explanation. He kept quiet, took the firing and went off.

At 10.30 a.m. all the officers would gather for a tea-break.

Now Mohabbat broke his silence. He said, "Kher sir, today I was late for PT. Actually what happened was I left my house well in time." He used to live in Model Town, a civilian area.

"On reaching the first crossing, the traffic was blocked. I moved my bike forward and found a Tonga had halted and the Tongawala was dancing in front of the Tonga. I shouted at the Tongawala but he told me politely, 'Bhaisahab, I bought this horse from a wedding bajawala; at every crossing, it halts and does not move unless I dance in front of it."

Captain Kher was astonished and would not believe Mohabbat's story. At this point, Major Surat Singh interjected, "Kher, Mohabbat is telling the truth. I have been a passenger on that Tonga."

A Great Initiative of Bishember

39 Medium Quarter Guard's flowerbeds had no decorative brick lining. Usually the Defence Forces have no funds for these things. JCO Adjutant (JA) Bishember got a mouthful and had to do something on his own.

One fine day, Sub Bishember Singh loaded 15 Khalsajis in a three-ton and moved for reconnaissance of the construction sites. At a lucrative-looking site, the men dismounted after due consideration and posting lookouts. Bishember ordered loading of the bricks. When the truck was almost full of bricks, the bloody contractor appeared and Bishember on his part maintained his posture and composure.

Contractor asked, "What the hell are you doing?"

Bishember said, "Sir, these men are weak. They have come last in ammo-loading competition. They are under punishment and have to practice load /unload."

Subedar Bishember ordered load/unload five times in the presence of the contractor. The contractor believed the man and left the site.

On the sixth time, when the truck was full, Bishember did not order 'unload'; instead shouted 'mount and move'.

The Case of Missing Bulldozer

At Jhansi, a Self-Propelled (SP) Regiment reported to Brigade HQ that its bulldozer had been stolen. An extensive search in Jhansi Cantonment and town yielded no results. The SP Regiment suspected the hand of 39 Medium Singhs.

Subedar Major (SM) Ram Singh was an old timer from 16 Sikh Frontier Force days, 39's original unit which had the honour of getting upgraded to Artillery.

He personally went and requested the neighbouring SP unit SM for a dozer to level the parade ground for ADM inspection as it was in bad shape. SM SP Regiment: "*Kaisa CO Sahib say baat karna ji*." And this was after the SP regiment SM owed Ram Singh a favour from before.

Ram Singh reminded him, during the inspection, "Your vehicle had met with an accident and I had substituted my vehicle with changed markings to save your skin. I had also sent help to load your gun ammo. I did not tell you, CO *Sahib se puchana*."

And that was the end of conversation between the two SMs and Ram Singh left in a huff.

Subsequently Adm inspection of 39 Medium was a success and SM Ram Singh received kudos for it.

In the meantime, the dozer was nowhere to be found and things were reaching a critical stage for the SP unit. The Brigade Commander came to 39 Medium and spoke to SM Ram Singh seeking his help. Ram Singh narrated the uncouth behaviour of the SM of SP Regiment. The SM was called and he was made to apologise. The Commander requested SM Ram Singh to return the dozer. The Commander himself was very curious and asked Ram Singh where the dozer was as the story of the missing dozer had taken epic proportions in the brigade.

SM Ram Singh said, "Sahibji jis *stage se kal aap ne parade ka salute leya,* o day thallay duubya paya ha*i*."(It's buried under the stage from which you took the salute for the parade yesterday).

How he managed to steal the dozer from SP MT (military transport) Park is a leaf out of military planning and adaptability.

From the moment he came back after meeting the SM from SP unit, Ram Singh enacted the operation "*Chack dozer*." Immediately a khalsaji was dispatched to reconnaissance the location of the bulldozer and it was identified as parked on the extreme left of the SP unit MT Park. The MT Park was guarded by one sentry with a shift change every three hours and this was the case at night too.

The security was a bit lax due to Jhansi being a peace station and far away from the border. Armed with this information, Ram Singh set up a four-man team to work in twos. The plan was to grab the dozer at 0100 hrs and use the dozer all night to level the parade ground and return it before sunrise, undetected. As the clock struck 0100 hrs, a small controlled fire was lit by the two-men team and a small fire cracker was set off to grab the attention of the sentry. The moment the sentry left his post to check the incident, another two-man team sneaked into the MT Park and ran towards the dozer. The plan worked beautifully till the Khalsaji tried to start the dozer. To their shock, it didn't start and it was dead. On quick inspection, it was found that there was no battery in the machine and hence nobody could steal it. It was impossible! The plan had to be abandoned for this night.

The same plan was enacted the next day with the Khalsas carrying the battery with them. This time the plan worked beautifully and the dozer was out, undetected. Full use of the dozer was made to clear the ground but a critical error took place. The Khalsas misjudged the timing to stop work to return the dozer before sunrise. An attempt to return it now, especially after sun rise, would have resulted in being caught redhanded. Instead it was decided to bury the dozer, build a stage over it for the parade salute and face the consequences as they came.

Remembering EBR Shankar Lal

In 39 Medium Regiment during Division Games meet they couldn't find a feather-weight Khalsa for the feather-weight boxing bout category. All they had to do was to put up a boxer and they were assured of a point. Forfeiting the bout meant losing a point. Winning was not necessary.

Shankar Lal was the only hope and was pumped up to fight. He was assured that the towel would be thrown in in the initial stage itself to save him from getting a beating.

The bout started. Shankar Lal started running in the ring with the other boxer chasing him and finally managing to hit him. Poor Shankar Lal shouted, "*Mat maaro, ma EBR Shankar Lal hoon. Ak point kay leya khada hoon bas.*" (Don't hit me, I am Shankar Lal EBR and I am only here standing to gain a point.)

EBR is Equipment Boot Repairer (cobbler).

Chhind Singh

39 Medium Regiment had gone to Delhi for firing in Tagulakabad Ranges. Chhind Singh was signal NCO. He was laying the line from OP to gun position.

Major AK Kher was the officiating CO After midnight he heard a loud cry of 'Sat Ari Akal." On coming out, he saw Chhind's turban back to front and his face and arms full of bruises.

Major Kher asked, "*Chhind, kitney mar gaya*?" (How many dead?)

Chhind reported, "Sahib, nobody is dead. Two men walking were wounded and repairable locally, one-ton upside down, windscreen damaged, one rifle bent, petrol from tank leaked."

In the range, a civilian truck had caused an accident and run away.

Major Kher, after a thought, ordered, "Vehicle will be on road by tomorrow first light. Petrol, I will deal; rifle barrel bent, I will deal. Now get lost."

Next morning the vehicle was produced for Major Kher's inspection; it was freshly painted and had a new windscreen.

Under correct motivation, this is the power men had to pull off the impossible and deliver under tough conditions.

Gunner Salwant Singh

He was a young gunner from RS. Pura, Jammu, a gun number of a Gun detachment of 122 Medium Battery, 39 Medium Regiment and was on practice camp in Delhi ranges for live firing exercise. Major AK Kher was sitting outside the Regiment Command post. While firing was going on, Adjutant Major Dhasmana came running out of the Command Post and said, "Sir, there has been a major accident in 122 Medium Battery."

Major Kher rushed to 122 Medium Battery and was aghast to see Gunner Salwant's right arm caught between the recoil and jacket of the gun barrel near the loading chamber. The recoil was jammed and the barrel was extreamly hot. Salwant Singh's Gun No. 1 was standing with a saw to chop his arm off to save his life.

Major AK Kher reported to CO that Gun No. 4 of 122 Medium Battery was out of action and ordered gun No. 3 to fire an extra round to compensate for the out-of-action gun.

Now it was a race against time to save Salwant. Major

Kher assured Salwant that nothing would happen to his arm and only asked of him to hold on and maintain courage. He then shouted out for his favourite gun fitter CHM Ram Singh. But Ram was not to be found. A search party was sent but they could not locate him. Meanwhile, ice cold water was poured on Salwant's arm to protect it from getting roasted due to the hot gun barrel.

In the meantime, Major Kher called for a Kraz from the wagon lines and placed it right in front of the said gun. The winch was opened and fastened to the muzzle of the gun. The GPO constantly announced on his loud hailer for CHM Ram Singh to rush to Gun No. 4 from wherever he was.

Finally Ram Singh showed up and responded that he was having loose motions and relieving himself. Major Kher ordered them to level the gun barrel by slowly tightening the winch and ordered Ram to release the recoil holding nut. The team made the barrel slowly slip back by a few inches, keeping the tension with the winch.

Salwant's arm came out intact with only some burns.

Salwant had requested his No. 1 to let him fire the round and had promised rum for the detachment. When the gun fired, with the jump of the gun, Salwant lost balance. He did not move his hand from the firing lever and his arm was caught between the recoil and barrel.

The knowledge of dismantling guns for glacier operations came in handy to save Salwant's arm from being amputated that day.

Brasstacks

In the final stages of Operation Brasstacks, the Command Post of 39 Medium Regiment along with 122 and 123 Medium Batteries was deployed near Sardarshahar, Rajasthan, along with other units of 18 Infantry Div. The final objective of the attacking force was to overrun the defences of Sardarshahar. To achieve that objective, the enemy forces had to pass through 39 Medium gun area, simulating the enemy's Infantry assault.

Upon commencement of attack, the umpires declared the gun area overrun by the enemy Infantry.

This easy declaration by the umpires upset Subedar Sardool Singh and the men of 39 Medium. The umpire party and some officers of the Infantry were caught by the men of Sub Sardool Singh and were on the verge of getting beaten up.

Major AK Kher was 2IC, reached the spot and took the umpires to the guns and showed them how 130 mm functions in direct shooting role. He then asked them to decide if such guns could be overrun just like that with 10 LMGs in defence as well, covering the area. After some consideration, the umpires declared the attack unsuccessful. During this melee, Major Kher heard the attacking Infantry men shouting, "*Oye yaa to Kher saab ki unit hai.*" All of their officers came forward and started hugging Major Kher. These attacking troops turned out to be from 18 Kumaon Regiment and were Major Kher's buddies from Siachen Glacier .39 Medium guns had fired in support of 18 Kumaon in 1985 for Operation Meghdoot.

Thereafter Major Kher took all the officers to his tent and offered them tea and biscuits. It was also found that these troops had not eaten anything for the last three days. Major Kher called in one of the senior JCOs of 123 Medium Battery and directed him to prepare a quick meal of *daal-chawal* for the 18 Kumaon men. All 18 Kumaon men were fed in the gun area and finally they were allowed to move forward towards their final objective, in keeping with the spirit of the exercise. This all happened past midnight. In the morning, Major Kher was questioned by higherups as to why the enemy troops were fed unit rations!

Long after Retirement of AK Kher

Lt Col AK Kher was standing with Lt Gen HK Bharadwaj, his first Commander at Amritsar in 1968, and Major General LS Lehl of Bangladesh fame, an ex-39 at this Artillery reunion organised by the School of Artillery Devlali, Nashik.

They were joined by Lt Gen Bhupender Singh, OIC TEC cell at AHQ. After exchanging pleasantries, he then went on to narrate an interesting story from the time when he was commanding a Brigade in Uri. He was visiting a Sikh LI Battalion, moving from picket to picket and was introduced to a Singh by the CO of Sikh LI.

The Singh in this story was on sentry duty and manning an LMG post at night. The Post Commander was a Subedar and while checking duties at night, he found this Singh sleeping and very tactfully removed his LMG and hid it in his own bunker.

Next morning, while checking duties at 'stand to', the Subedar found the same Singh manning the post with an LMG.

Puzzled, he went back to his bunker and found the LMG he had picked up last night, still there intact. Visibly perplexed, the Subedar went back to Singh and asked how it was possible and demanded an explanation.

Singh told him, "Sahibji you don't like me; you are always after me. When I woke up from my nap, I found the LMG gone and I sought Wahe Guru's help as I knew you will make my life hell. The only solution I could think of was to cross the wire obstacles, the minefield and pick up the Pakistani sentry's LMG as he was also sleeping. Then, at night, I put the Indian marking on the weapon."

At that time, on hearing this, Brigadier Bhupinder was delighted to meet this Singh and decorated him with the Sena Medal on the spot.

Meanwhile, during the ongoing conversation between the

groups, two Singh Havaldars came to the group and saluted the General in uniform. They came forward and touched Lt Col AK Kher's feet after a *joshwala* 'Sat Sri Akal.' When they were leaving, Lt Gen Bhupender called them and asked them why they had touched Lt Col AK Kher's feet as the Khalsa's normally do not do this as a practice.

Both the Singhs came to attention and said, "*Sahib, yeh Kher Sahib hai, hamara CO sahib. Laddai mein hamare se agay chaltey hain, aur hum Sahib ke peechay peechay turdey hain.*"(In war, he moves ahead and we keep running behind him to keep up.)

Lt Gen Bhupender came to attention and saluted Lt Col AK Kher and said, 'Kher Sahib, even I have not earned such respect."

'Gladiators live in obscurity, Generals live in fame.'

—Lt Col AK Kher

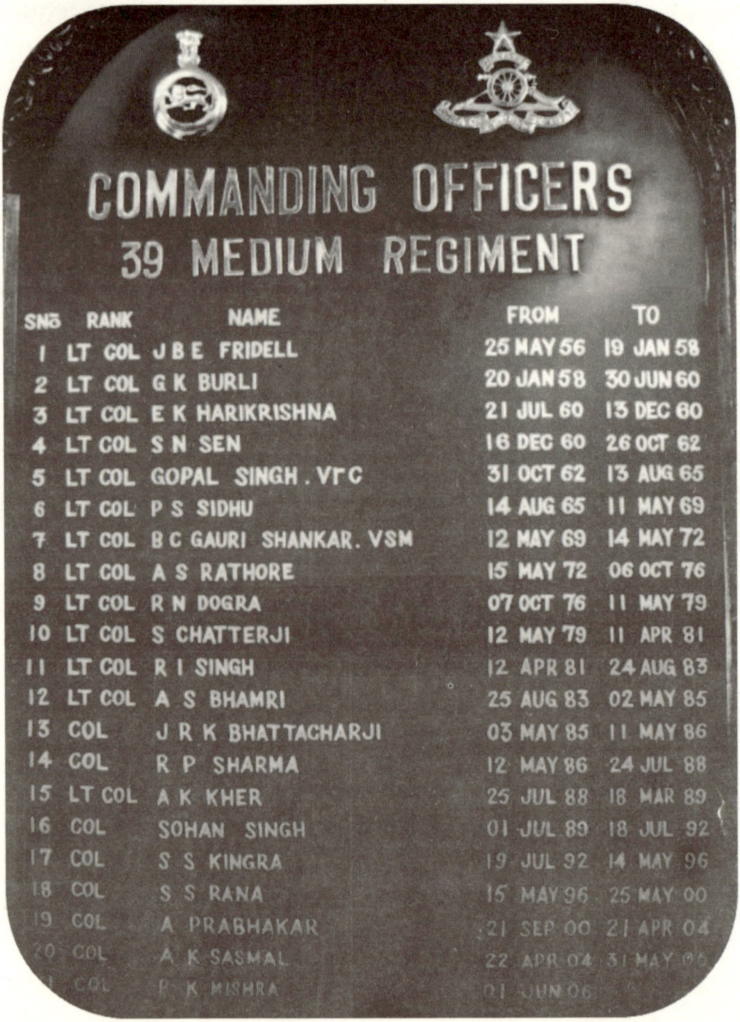

COMMANDING OFFICERS
39 MEDIUM REGIMENT

SNo	RANK	NAME	FROM	TO
1	LT COL	J B E FRIDELL	25 MAY 56	19 JAN 58
2	LT COL	G K BURLI	20 JAN 58	30 JUN 60
3	LT COL	E K HARIKRISHNA	21 JUL 60	13 DEC 60
4	LT COL	S N SEN	16 DEC 60	26 OCT 62
5	LT COL	GOPAL SINGH. VrC	31 OCT 62	13 AUG 65
6	LT COL	P S SIDHU	14 AUG 65	11 MAY 69
7	LT COL	B C GAURI SHANKAR. VSM	12 MAY 69	14 MAY 72
8	LT COL	A S RATHORE	15 MAY 72	06 OCT 76
9	LT COL	R N DOGRA	07 OCT 76	11 MAY 79
10	LT COL	S CHATTERJI	12 MAY 79	11 APR 81
11	LT COL	R I SINGH	12 APR 81	24 AUG 83
12	LT COL	A S BHAMRI	25 AUG 83	02 MAY 85
13	COL	J R K BHATTACHARJI	03 MAY 85	11 MAY 86
14	COL	R P SHARMA	12 MAY 86	24 JUL 88
15	LT COL	A K KHER	25 JUL 88	18 MAR 89
16	COL	SOHAN SINGH	01 JUL 89	18 JUL 92
17	COL	S S KINGRA	19 JUL 92	14 MAY 96
18	COL	S S RANA	15 MAY 96	25 MAY 00
19	COL	A PRABHAKAR	21 SEP 00	21 APR 04
20	COL	A K SASMAL	22 APR 04	31 MAY 06
21	COL	R K MISHRA	01 JUN 06	

Lt Col AK Kher's Farewell from 39 Medium

Long after retirement at Udhampur in December 2008

Lt Col AK Kher with CO Col PK Mishra

With men of the unit

Signing of 39 Medium Unit book

Welcome at JCO's Mess

Gun Drill Demo

Once upon a time there was a Sikh warrior

With Hav Maj Attar Singh and family at his house in 2017

L/Hav Baldev Singh with his family in 2017

While in Service, Baldev Singh was Lt Col Kher's buddy for 10 years

39 Medium Regiment Diamond Jubilee at Firozpur, 2017

Travel to China

□

Index

1. Section: The smallest unit of army is called 'Section'; it contains 10-11 soldiers.

2. Platoon: It consists three sections.

3. Company: It consists of three platoons. Its chief is called Company Commander.

4. Battalion: Has 4 Rifle company, one support and one HQ company. Usually commanded by a Colonel/Lt Col.

5. Infantry Brigade: Consists of three Battalions. Commanded by a Brigadier.

6. Artillery Brigade: Consists of three Field Regiments, one Medium Regiment, one Light Battery of 12 Mortar and one SATA (Surface Acquisition Target Battery)

7. Division: Usually commanded by a Major General.

8. Corps: It is commanded by a Lieutenant General.

Rank Structure

9. Non-commissioned Rank:

- Sepoy
- Lance Naik (L/Nk)
- Naik (Nk)
- Havildar (Hav) • BHM (Batallion Hav Major)
- CHM (Company Hav Major)
- RPH (Regimental Police Hav)

10. Junior Commissioned Officer (JCO)

- Naib Subedar (N/Sub)
- Subedar (Sub)
- Subedar Adjutant or JA
- Subedar Major (SM)

11. Commissioned Ranks

- 2/Lieutenant (2/LT); now discontinued
- Lieutenant (LT)
- Captain (Capt)
- Major (Maj) Brigade Major (BM)
- Lieutenant Colonel (Lt Col)
- Colonel (Col)
- Brigadier (Brig)
- Major General (Maj Gen)
- Lieutenant General (Lt Gen)
- General (Gen) Army Chief
- General (Gen) Chief of Defence Staff (CDS)

Awards and Decorations of Indian Armed Forces mentioned in this book:

War Time Gallantry awards

- Param Vir Chakra (PVC)
- Maha Vir Chakra (MVC)
- Vir Chakra (VrC)
- Sena Medal (SM)

Peace-time Distinguished Service medals

- Param Vishisht Seva Medal (PVSM)
- Ati Vishisht Seva Medal (AVSM)
- Vishisht Seva Medal (VSM)

Mention in Dispatches

In order to recognise distinguished and meritorious service in operational areas and acts of gallantry which are not of a sufficiently high order to warrant the grant of gallantry awards.